Praise for
Primal

"Mark weaves us through the Great Commandment with insights that are both winsome and wise, piquing both curiosity and conviction. He calls us to a discipleship free of the trappings of shriveled self-concern, drawing us to give ourselves, with abandon, to others as we heed Jesus' call to love God above all. This book will fuel clarity of call and persevering strength for those who will journey in obedience to the Gospel—in its wholeness of justice, mercy, and faithfulness—for a lifetime."

—GARY HAUGEN, president and CEO of International Justice
Mission and author of *Good News About Injustice, Terrify
No More,* and *Just Courage*

"Too many of us are doing life at an unsustainable pace and losing sight of our first love. In his new book, *Primal,* Mark Batterson invites you to rediscover the reality of Christ and His passions. This book will challenge you, push you, and stretch you. You will walk away righteously aggravated, but catapulted into action."

—CRAIG GROESCHEL, senior pastor of LifeChurch.tv

"Mark, I'm with you. It's time for believers to be more. Let's hear the voice of God and be that holy, passionate fire that we are called to be. It's the primal way."

—SHAUN ALEXANDER, 2005 NFL MVP, acclaimed speaker, and
author of award-winning book *Touch Down Alexander*

PRIMAL

PRIMAL

A Quest for the Lost Soul of Christianity

MARK
BATTERSON

Best-selling author of *In a Pit with a Lion on a Snowy Day*

MULTNOMAH
BOOKS

PRIMAL
PUBLISHED BY MULTNOMAH BOOKS
12265 Oracle Boulevard, Suite 200
Colorado Springs, Colorado 80921

The names of some individuals whose stories are told in this book have been changed to protect their privacy.

ISBN 978-1-60142-131-9
ISBN 978-1-60142-257-6 (electronic)

Published in association with Eames Literary Services, Nashville, Tennessee.

Library of Congress Cataloging-in-Publication Data
Batterson, Mark.
    Primal : a quest for the lost soul of Christianity / Mark Batterson. — 1st ed.
        p. cm.
    ISBN 978-1-60142-131-9—ISBN 978-1-60142-257-6 (electronic)
    1. God—Worship and love. 2. Christianity—Essence, genius, nature. I. Title.
    BV4817.B28 2010
    280'.4—dc22
                                        2009039798

Printed in the United States of America
2009—First Edition

10 9 8 7 6 5 4 3 2 1

To my grandparents Elmer and Alene Johnson...
Your prayers outlive you.

CONTENTS

Two Thousand Stairs

The farther backward you look, the further forward you
are likely to see.

—WINSTON CHURCHILL

We hopped on a double-decker bus and headed toward the heart
of Rome. Lora and I had spent a year planning the trip, but
nothing prepares you to stand in the very place where Caesars ruled an
empire or gladiators battled to the death. As we walked the Via Sacra, we
were stepping on the same two-thousand-year-old stones that conquer-
ing armies marched on. Of course, I'm guessing they weren't licking
gelatos. Our three days in the Eternal City went by far too fast. And I
wish we hadn't waited until our fifteenth anniversary to take the trip.

Few places on earth are as historic or romantic as Rome. We thor-
oughly enjoyed strolling the ancient streets, people-watching in the piaz-
zas, and eating leisurely meals at sidewalk cafés. And like good tourists, we
also hit all the must-see travel-book destinations. We threw pennies over
our shoulders into the Trevi Fountain, enjoyed an unplugged concert by
an electric guitarist outside the Colosseum one moonlit evening, and took
a three-hour tour of St. Peter's Basilica. And all the sites lived up to their
travel-book billing. But one of the unexpected highlights of our trip was
an unplanned visit to a rather nondescript church off the beaten path. It
wasn't referenced in our travel guides. And if it hadn't been right around
the corner from our hotel, we would never have discovered it. The Church

of San Clemente was named after the fourth pope, who was martyred for his faith. According to legend, anchors were tied around his ankles and he was thrown into the Black Sea.

From the outside, the church appeared weather-beaten and time-worn. But the frescoes, statues, and altars on the inside were remarkably well preserved. We quietly explored every nook and cranny of that twelfth-century church. Then we discovered that for five extra euros we could take an underground tour. As was the case with many of the ruins we visited in Rome, there were several layers of history in the same place. The Romans had a habit of building things on top of things. Some emperors, for example, would tear down their predecessor's palace and build their own palace right on top of it. Such was the case with the Church of San Clemente. The twelfth-century church was built over a fourth-century church. And beneath the fourth-century church were cat-acombs where second-century Christians secretly worshiped God before the legalization of Christianity by Constantine in 313.

I'll never forget my descent down that flight of stairs. The air became damp, and we could hear underground springs. We carefully navigated each step as we lost some of our light. And our voices echoed off the low ceiling and narrow walkway. Almost like the wardrobe in the Chronicles of Narnia, that flight of stairs was like a portal to a different time, a different place. It was as if those stairs took us back two thousand years in time. With each step, a layer of history was stripped away until all that was left was Christianity in all its primal glory.

As we navigated those claustrophobic catacombs, I was overcome by the fact that I was standing in a place where my spiritual ancestors risked everything, even their lives, to worship God. And I felt a profound mixture of gratitude and conviction. I live in a first-world country in the twenty-first century. And I'm grateful for the freedoms and blessings I enjoy because of where and when I live. But when you're standing in an ancient catacomb, the comforts you enjoy make you uncomfortable. The things you complain about are convicting. And some of the sacrifices you've made for the cause of Christ might not even qualify under a second-century definition.

As I tried to absorb the significance of where I was, I couldn't help but wonder if our generation has conveniently forgotten how inconvenient it can be to follow in the footsteps of Christ. I couldn't help but wonder if we have diluted the truths of Christianity and settled for superficialities. I couldn't help but wonder if we have accepted a form of Christianity that is more educated but less powerful, more civilized but less compassionate, more acceptable but less authentic than that which our spiritual ancestors practiced.

Over the last two thousand years, Christianity has evolved in lots of ways. We've come out of the catacombs and built majestic cathedrals with all the bells and steeples. Theologians have given us creeds and canons. Churches have added pews and pulpits, hymnals and organs, committees and liturgies. And the IRS has given us 501(c)(3) status. And there is nothing inherently wrong with any of those things. But none of those things is primal. And I wonder, almost like the Roman effect of building things on top of things, if the accumulated layers of Christian traditions and institutions have unintentionally obscured what lies beneath.

I'm not suggesting that we categorically dismiss all those evolutions as unbiblical. Most of them are simply abiblical. There aren't precedents for them in Scripture, but they don't contradict biblical principles either. I'm certainly not demonizing postmodern forms of worship. After all, the truth must be reincarnated in every culture in every generation. And I am personally driven by the conviction that there are ways of doing church that no one has thought of yet. But two thousand years of history raises this question: when all of the superficialities are stripped away, what is the primal essence of Christianity?

In the pages that follow, I want you to descend that flight of stairs with me. I want us to go underground. I want us to go back in time. Think of it as a quest for the lost soul of Christianity. And by the time you reach the last page, I hope you will have done more than rediscover Christianity in its most primal form. I hope you will have gone back to the primal faith *you* once had. Or more accurately, the primal faith that once had you.

THE FAR SIDE OF COMPLEXITY

My kids are at that stage in their mathematical journey where they are learning about prime numbers. That means that, as a parent, I am relearning about prime numbers (along with every other math concept I have long since forgotten). A prime number is a number that is divisible only by itself and the number 1. And while an infinitude of prime numbers exists, the only even prime is the number 2.

Certain truths qualify as prime truths. Bible-believing, God-fearing, Christ-loving Christians will disagree about a variety of doctrinal issues until Jesus returns, whether that be pre-, mid-, or post-Tribulation. That is why we have hundreds of different denominations. But prime truths have an indivisible quality to them. And chief among them—the even prime, if you will—is what Jesus called the most important commandment. We call it the Great Commandment. It could also be called the Primal Commandment because it is of first importance.

> *Love the Lord your God with all your heart and with all your soul and with all your mind and with all your strength.*[1]

Jesus was a genius. He had the ability to simplify complex spiritual truths in unforgettable and irrefutable ways. I'm afraid we tend to do the opposite. We complicate Christianity. That religious tendency to over-complicate simple spiritual truths traces all the way back to a sect of Judaism known as the Pharisees. Over the span of hundreds of years, the Pharisees compiled a comprehensive list of religious dos and don'ts. Six hundred and thirteen, to be exact.[2] Jesus peeled them back with one primal statement. When all of the rules and regulations, all of the traditions and institutions, all of the liturgies and methodologies are peeled back, what's left is the Great Commandment. It is Christianity in its most primal form.

Sounds so simple, doesn't it? If only it were as simple as it sounds.

Oliver Wendell Holmes, former chief justice of the Supreme Court, once made a perceptive distinction between two kinds of simplicity: simplicity on the near side of complexity and simplicity on the far side of complexity. He said, "I would not give a fig for simplicity on the near side of complexity."

Many Christians settle for simplicity on the near side of complexity. Their faith is only mind deep. They know *what* they believe, but they don't know *why* they believe what they believe. Their faith is fragile because it has never been tested intellectually or experientially. Near-side Christians have never been in the catacombs of doubt or suffering, so when they encounter questions they cannot answer or experiences they cannot explain, it causes a crisis of faith. For far-side Christians, those who have done their time in the catacombs of doubt or suffering, unanswerable questions and unexplainable experiences actually result in a heightened appreciation for the mystery and majesty of a God who does not fit within the logical constraints of the left brain. Near-side Christians, on the other hand, lose their faith before they've really found it.

Simplicity on the near side of complexity goes by another name: *spiritual immaturity.* And that's not the kind of simplicity I'm advocating. God calls us to simplicity on the far side of complexity. For that matter, He calls us to faith on the far side of doubt, joy on the far side of sorrow, and love on the far side of anger. So how do we get there? Well, there are no easy answers or quick fixes. It involves unlearning and relearning everything we know. It involves deconstructing and reconstructing everything we do. It involves the painstaking process of rediscovering and reimagining the primal essence of Christianity. But the result is simplicity on the far side of complexity. And that is where this flight of stairs will take us if we have the courage to go underground.

THE PRIMAL PROBLEM

It goes without saying that Christianity has a perception problem. At the heart of the problem is the simple fact that Christians are more known for what we're *against* than what we're *for*. But the real problem isn't perception. We as Christians are often quick to point out what's wrong with our culture. And we certainly need the moral courage to stand up for what's right in the face of what's wrong. I live in the bastion of political correctness, where it is wrong to say that something is wrong. And that's wrong. If we have to choose between political correctness and biblical correctness, we must choose biblical correctness every time. But before confronting what's wrong with our culture, we need to be humble enough, honest enough, and courageous enough to repent of what's wrong with us.

I pastor a church in Washington DC that is nearly 70 percent single twenty-somethings. Unfortunately, our demographics are an anomaly. By and large, twenty-somethings are leaving the church at an alarming rate. According to some statistics, 61 percent of twenty-somethings who grew up going to church will quit going to church in their twenties.[3] And the temptation is to ask this question: what's wrong with this generation? But that is the wrong question. The right question is this: what's wrong with the church?

My answer is simply this: we're not great at the Great Commandment. In too many instances, we're not even good at it.

That, I believe, is our primal problem. That is the lost soul of Christianity. If Jesus said that loving God with all our heart, soul, mind, and strength is the most important commandment, then doesn't it logically follow that we ought to spend an inordinate amount of our time and energy trying to understand it and obey it? We can't afford to be merely good at the Great Commandment. We've got to be great at the Great Commandment.

The quest for the lost soul of Christianity begins with rediscovering what it means to love God with all our heart, soul, mind, and strength. Jesus used those four kaleidoscopic words to describe four dimensions of love. And there is certainly overlap among them. It's hard to know where loving God with your heart ends and loving God with your soul begins. But one thing is sure: loving God in one way isn't enough. It's not enough to love God with *just* your heart or soul or mind or strength. We are called, even commanded, to love Him in all four ways. Think of it as love to the fourth power.

So the quest begins with rediscovery. But it ends with reimagination. Some truths can be deduced via left-brain logic. Others are better induced via right-brain imagination. Love falls into the latter category. So what follows is not a strict exposition of the Great Commandment. It's a reimagination of the four primal elements detailed by Jesus in the Great Commandment:

> *The heart of Christianity is primal compassion.*
> *The soul of Christianity is primal wonder.*
> *The mind of Christianity is primal curiosity.*
> *And the strength of Christianity is primal energy.*

The descent down this flight of stairs into primal Christianity will be convicting at points, but the end result will be a renewed love for God that is full of genuine compassion, infinite wonder, insatiable curiosity, and boundless energy. Anything less is not enough. It's not just unful-filling, it's also unfaithful. The quest is not complete until it results in catacomb-like convictions that go beyond conventional logic. The goal is a love that, as our spiritual ancestors understood, is worth living for and dying for.

THE WAY FORWARD

My aim in this book is to take you to new places intellectually and spir-itually so that you discover new ways of loving God. But I also hope this book takes you back to a primal place where God loved you and you loved God. And that's all that mattered.

I've discovered that when I've lost my way spiritually, the way forward is often backward. That is what we experience when we celebrate Com-munion, isn't it? Communion is a pilgrimage back to the foot of the cross. And going back to that most primal place helps us find our way forward. So before going forward, let me encourage you to go backward. Go back to that place where God opened your eyes and broke your heart with compassion for others. Go back to that place where the glory of God flooded your soul and left you speechless with wonder. Go back to that place where thoughts about God filled your mind with holy curiosity. Go back to that place where a God-given dream caused a rush of adrenaline that filled you with supernatural energy.

Every year our entire church staff goes on a pilgrimage to the Cata-lyst Conference in Atlanta, Georgia. During one of the sessions this past year, our team was sitting in the balcony of the Gwinnett Center listening to my friend and the pastor of LifeChurch.tv, Craig Groeschel. And he asked this question: "Does your heart break for the things that break the heart of God?"

I felt a tremendous sense of conviction when Craig asked that question. As I sat in that balcony, surrounded by twelve thousand other leaders, I heard the still, small voice of the Holy Spirit. The Spirit said to my spirit in His kind yet convicting voice, *Mark, what happened to the college kid who used to pace the chapel balcony seeking My face?*

There are few things I *hate more* or *appreciate more* than the conviction of the Holy Spirit. It is so painful. But it is so necessary. And I'm so grateful that God loves me enough to break me where I need to be broken. Can I make an observation? You cannot listen to just half of what the Holy Spirit has to say. It's a package deal. If you aren't willing to listen to everything He has to say, you won't hear anything He has to say. If you tune out His convicting voice, you won't hear His comforting voice or guiding voice either. As I was seated in that balcony, the Holy Spirit reminded me of the raw spiritual intensity I once had. He revealed how calloused my heart had become. And I realized that I had somehow lost my soul while serving God. And it wrecked me.

Does your heart break for the things that break the heart of God?

If it doesn't, you need to repent. And that's what I did that day. Our team is typically the first to hit the exit after the last session at conferences because, quite frankly, the first one to the restaurant wins. And we had reservations at one of my favorite restaurants, P.F. Chang's. Love their lettuce wraps and spare ribs. I could almost taste them. But we couldn't leave until we brought closure to what God was doing in the depths of our souls. So we delayed our reservation, found a conference room, and spent some time crying, confessing, and praying as a team. I think we were the last ones to leave the auditorium.

In the providence of God, I happened to be scheduled to speak at my alma mater in Springfield, Missouri, the next week. So a few days later I found myself in the chapel balcony where I had logged hundreds of hours pacing back and forth seeking God. It was during prayer times in that balcony when my heart began to break for the things that break the heart of God. It was there that God began to shape my soul to seek Him. It was there that God began to fill my mind with God ideas. It was in that balcony that God energized me by giving me a God-sized vision for my life.

Returning to that chapel balcony fifteen years later, I realized that in many ways I had become a paid professional Christian. My heart didn't beat as strongly as it once did. My pulse didn't quicken in the presence of God like it once had. So God took me back to a very primal place. And the Holy Spirit lovingly reminded me that the college kid with a huge heart for God was still somewhere inside me. I knew that getting back what I once had meant getting back to basics. It meant doing what I had once done. It meant rediscovering and reimagining what it means to love God with all my heart, soul, mind, and strength. And somewhere along the way, in my personal quest for my lost soul, I found it. Climbing those stairs into that chapel balcony was like descending those stairs into that ancient catacomb. God gave me back the compassion, wonder, curiosity, and energy I once had, along with an even greater appreciation for what I had lost and found.

Is there a personal catacomb somewhere in your past? A place where you met God and God met you? A place where your heart broke with compassion? A place where your soul was filled with wonder? A place where your mind was filled with holy curiosity? A place where you were energized by a God-ordained dream? Maybe it was a sermon that became more than a sermon. God birthed something supernatural in your spirit. Maybe it was a mission trip or retreat. And you swore you'd never be the same again. Or maybe it was a dream or a vow or a decision you made at an altar. My prayer is that this book will take you down two thousand stairs back to that primal place—the place where loving God with all your heart, soul, mind, and strength is all that matters.

The quest for the lost soul of Christianity begins there.

PART 1

THE HEART
OF CHRISTIANITY

2

The Tribe of the Transplanted

If we could read the secret history of our enemies, we should find in each man's life sorrow and suffering enough to disarm all hostility.

—HENRY WADSWORTH LONGFELLOW

Several years ago I had the privilege of attending the National Prayer Breakfast held annually at the Washington Hilton Hotel. The breakfast is a bipartisan gathering of leaders from all branches of government and both houses of Congress as well as delegations of leaders from foreign countries. The speaker that year was Bill Frist. Prior to his tenure in the U.S. Senate, Dr. Frist performed more than 150 heart transplants as a thoracic surgeon. During his remarks, he talked in reverent tones about the moment when a heart has been grafted into a new body and all the surgical team can do is wait in hopes that it will begin to beat. At that point he stopped speaking in medical terms and starting speaking in spiritual terms. He almost seemed at a loss for words as he described that miraculous moment when a heart beats in a new body for the first time. He called it a *mystery*.

Heart transplants are a marvel of modern medicine, but the heart goes way beyond what medicine can explain or understand. It is more than a physical pump. It doesn't just circulate five thousand quarts of blood through sixty thousand miles of blood vessels day in and day out. The heart has a mind of its own. Studies suggest that the heart secretes its own brainlike hormones and has cellular memory. So a heart transplant isn't just physical, it's metaphysical. Heart transplant recipients don't just receive a new organ, they receive cellular memories.

In his book *A Man After His Own Heart,* Charles Siebert shares a scientific yet poetic depiction of a heart transplant he observed at NewYork-Presbyterian Hospital in New York City. Not long after, Siebert attended an annual banquet for transplant recipients, and he was deeply moved by their profound appreciation for life. They spoke in reverent tones about the second chance at life they had been given. They humbly acknowledged their responsibility to honor the donors. And many of them talked about new desires that accompanied their new hearts.

Siebert concluded—and his research is backed up by numerous medical studies—that transplant recipients don't just receive a new heart. Along with that new heart, they receive whole new sensory responses, cravings, and habits.

Siebert called this group of heart recipients "the tribe of the transplanted."

I will give you a new heart and put a new spirit in you; I will remove from you your heart of stone and give you a heart of flesh.[1]

COUP DE COMPASSION

A life may be filled with lots of amazing moments, but nothing even begins to compare with that miraculous moment when you give your heart to Christ. That single decision sets off a spiritual chain reaction with infinite implications. A new child is adopted into the family of God. A new name is written in the Lamb's Book of Life. And an old heart is exchanged for a new heart.

When you give your heart to Christ, Christ gives His heart to you. And you become a part of the tribe of the transplanted. That new heart gives you a new appreciation for life. You humbly acknowledge your responsibility to honor the donor. And the cellular memories that come with that transplanted heart give you whole new sensory responses, cravings, and habits. You literally feel different. Why? Because you feel what Christ feels. And chief among those sanctified emotions is compassion. Your heart begins to break for the things that break the heart of God. And that is the heart of what it means to love God with all your heart.

It is a sad commentary and sadder irony that Christians are often viewed as heartless. And I think it's because we've engaged our culture mind-first instead of heart-first. Let me explain. I believe that Scripture is the inspired Word of God, right down to the jot and tittle. That means that even word sequence is significant. And when Jesus reveals the four primal elements of love, the heart comes first. I'm afraid that the Western church has tried to engage our culture mind-first instead of heart-first. But minds often remain closed to truth until hearts have been opened by compassion. There is certainly a place for logical, left-brained explanations of faith. But compassion is the ultimate apologetic. There is no defense against it.

I've already detailed the perception problem that Christianity has. Now let me personalize the problem. The problem isn't Christianity at large. The problem is you and me. The problem is that we're not great at the Great Commandment. Or in terms of the heart, we're not as compassionate as we could be or should be. That's the bad news. But here's the good news: Although you may be part of the problem, you can become part of the solution. You can change the face of Christianity, but it will require more than a face-lift. It starts with a change of heart.

Have you given your heart to Christ? All of it? If not, why not do it right here, right now? Stop reading and start praying. How? From your heart. God doesn't just hear your words. He hears your heart. He isn't impressed with words, but He is moved by a heartfelt prayer. And I promise you this: if you give your heart to Him, He'll give His heart to you. And when He does, you'll become part of this coup de compassion that started at the cross two thousand years ago. The compassion that Christ showed us at Calvary will become the driving force of your life.

NAMELESS NUMBERS

One of the most profound books I've ever read is *Man's Search for Meaning* by psychiatrist Viktor Frankl. In the book, Frankl documents his experiences as a Holocaust survivor. He was loaded onto an overcrowded railroad car with other Jewish prisoners and treated like an animal. When he arrived at his designated concentration camp, he was stripped of his clothing, his pictures, and his personal belongings. The Nazis even took away the prisoners' names and gave them numbers. Frankl was number 119,104.

Numbers are dehumanizing. Numbers are desensitizing.

Every year, fifteen million children die of starvation. When you break that number down, that is more than forty thousand children per day or nearly twenty-nine children every sixty seconds. But here's the problem: We don't know their names. We only know their number. And numbers are numbing. It's so easy for us to ignore suffering when it doesn't have a name or a face, isn't it?

Not long ago, Lora and I were in New York City for some meetings. During our downtime, we visited Ground Zero. In some ways, 9/11 seems like a false memory. It's hard to believe it actually happened. But when you visit Ground Zero, it almost seems like it happened yesterday. Lora and I quietly walked through the museum dedicated to the victims, and I'll never forget one exhibit. It contained the personal effects of one of the victims, Al Braca. His wallet, his keys, and a bank deposit slip dated September 11, 2001, were recovered from the wreckage. It's hard to describe, but somehow those personal effects personalized the tragedy for me.

Then I saw a display with the names of all the victims. As with seeing the names of fallen heroes engraved on the Vietnam Veterans Memorial, it turned a number into a name. Then a mosaic filled with pictures of victims put a face with a name. I happened to notice a swim cap along with the picture of a victim who had obviously run a triathlon. It impacted me deeply because I had just run a sprint triathlon with my son Parker, and I couldn't even imagine what I would have felt if my son had been one of the victims. I think it gave me a glimpse of what the heavenly Father must feel. The reason the heavenly Father identifies so deeply with our pain and suffering is that He watched His own Son suffer and die. His Son was the innocent victim of supreme injustice.

NOT OKAY

I recently attended a Civil Forum on Global Health sponsored by Saddleback Church and held at the Newseum in DC. The focus of the forum was on how churches can leverage their God-given resources to fight what Rick Warren calls the five global Goliaths: spiritual emptiness, self-serving leadership, extreme poverty, pandemic diseases, and rampant illiteracy.[2]

The event was timed to coincide with World AIDS Day, and we watched a video documenting the devastating effects of AIDS. Eight thousand people will die from AIDS today. Then, after all the stories and numbers and faces, the documentary posed this question: "Are you okay with this?"

United Nations health and food organizations calculate that twenty-five thousand people throughout the developing world die every day from starvation and malnutrition. Are you okay with this? There are a hundred thirty thousand children up for adoption at any given time in the United States, and millions more children worldwide are without families. Are you okay with this? A child dies from drinking contaminated water every twenty-one seconds.[3] Are you okay with this? That question can be and must be asked of all suffering and every injustice. Are you okay with this?

Most of us *are* okay with it. And we're okay with it simply because it's an issue without a name or a face. We've never held someone who is starving to death. No one in our family has needlessly died from contaminated water. We don't know anybody who has been kidnapped and sold into slavery. And none of our family members sleeps on the streets. But once the issue has a name and a face, it changes everything, doesn't it? God knows each of those names. God knows each of those faces. And it breaks His heart.

So let me ask the question: are you okay with this?

If you are in Christ and Christ is in you, you cannot be okay with suffering or injustice or starvation. Why? Because His heart is in you. And His heart beats for the suffering, the victim, the poor, and the needy. If you are a Christ follower, then you have been drafted into an army of compassion that knows no enemy but those things that break the heart of God. And it's not okay to not do something about them.

Sympathy Breakthroughs

One day while fighting in the Spanish Civil War, George Orwell had a face-to-face encounter with the enemy he'd come to kill. The famed English author had gone to fight fascism, but as an enemy soldier ran by him half naked, holding his pants up in the air, Orwell refused to shoot. He later reflected, "I did not shoot partly because of that detail about the trousers. I had come here to shoot at fascists; but a man who is holding up his trousers isn't a 'fascist,' he is visibly a fellow-creature, similar to yourself, and you don't feel like shooting at him."[4]

In his documentary on twentieth-century wars, Jonathan Glover refers to moments like this one as *sympathy breakthroughs.* Even in the context of war, there are acts of compassion that supersede the conflict. Most of the sympathy breakthroughs, according to Glover, are triggered by eye-to-eye contact, and that eye-to-eye contact short-circuits hand-to-hand combat. For what it's worth, according to the research of U.S. Army lieutenant colonel S. L. A. "Slam" Marshall, only 15 percent of World War II riflemen fired at the enemy during combat.[5]

Have you ever experienced a sympathy breakthrough? A moment when your inclination to hate was overcome by your will to love? A moment when proactive compassion overrode reactive anger? A moment when you cared more about someone else's pain than your own? Those are the moments when you recapture parts of your soul that you have lost. Those are the moments when you learn what it really means to love God with all your heart.

I recently received one of the most scathing e-mails ever to grace my in-box. The irony is that it came on the heels of what I thought was a great sermon (if I say so myself). I had preached my heart out, and I think I said what God wanted me to say. But no sooner had I gotten home than I got this e-mail laced with insults and attacks on my message and ministry. Now, before you throw me a pity party, let me say that I get far more complimentary e-mails than critical e-mails. And I've learned that criticism can be a healthy thing. If you don't let it harden your heart, you can actually learn something from it. And it keeps you grounded. Honestly, this e-mail reminded me that I preach for an audience of One. If I say what God wants me to say, then all the criticism in the world doesn't matter. And if I don't say what God wants me to say, then all the compliments in the world don't matter.

Having said that, let me say this: I was more than a little ticked off. Part of me wanted to preach another sermon for *that* audience of one—a hellfire and damnation sermon. The e-mail cursed me, and I wanted to curse back. Then, by the grace of God, I got an e-mail from the father of the person who had written the first e-mail. I discovered that his son had recently been in a tragic accident that killed four of his friends and he himself had barely survived. When I discovered that detail, it totally changed my perspective. Nothing is as disarming as discovering the suffering or sorrow in another person's past. Instead of going on the warpath, I made peace. Instead of reacting in anger, I reacted in compassion. Why? Because my heart broke for him the way God's heart must have broken for him when the accident happened. And to be perfectly honest, I'm not sure how I would have responded if I had gone through a similar experience.

I'm not saying you aren't responsible for your actions. And your pain doesn't give you a free pass to say whatever you want to say however you want to say it. But just as you are responsible for your actions, no matter how right or wrong they are, you are also responsible for your *reactions*. And compassion is always the right reaction. I'm not saying there isn't a place for rebuking, correcting, and exhorting. Sometimes that's the most loving thing you can do. But even those things can be and must be done in the spirit of compassion.

In my experience, it's much easier to act like a Christian than it is to react like one. Anyone can put on an act. But your reactions reveal what is really in your heart. And if you love God with all your heart, you won't just act like it. You'll react like it.

EQ

In his groundbreaking book *Emotional Intelligence,* Daniel Goleman asserts that IQ accounts for only 20 percent of the factors that lead to career success.[6] Goleman argues that emotional intelligence (EQ) is more important than IQ when it comes to work and the workplace. And as an employer, I would agree. I don't care about your GPA. The number-one thing we look for in potential hires at National Community Church is a sense of humor. If you can't laugh at my jokes, we can't work together. And I'm not joking. Seriously, life is too short and ministry is too hard. I want to work with people who know how to have fun. I want to work with people who have a great attitude. I want to work with people who don't just care about the work but who care about the people they work with.

Emotional intelligence is a multidimensional capacity that includes a wide range of abilities, including motivating oneself, persisting in the face of opposition, controlling emotional impulses, and regulating moods. But there is one dimension of emotional intelligence that Goleman says is absolutely foundational: empathy. Empathy is feeling what another person feels. And it's not just a dimension of emotional intelligence, it's a dimension of spiritual intelligence (SQ).

As we grow in our love relationship with God, we begin to empathize with God. We feel what He feels. Then we begin to sympathize with others. We experience sympathy breakthroughs as we see the image of God in others. And when those empathetic feelings turn into compassionate actions, they set off chain reactions with eternal ramifications.

Don't underestimate the spiritual significance of even one act of compassion done in the name of Christ. That one act of Spirit-prompted compassion can change the course of history. That is precisely what happened in an Egyptian dungeon three thousand years ago.

But before I share the story, let me share a little backstory. Consider the story of Joseph through the filter of emotional intelligence. As a teenager, Joseph had a zero EQ. He wasn't just emotionally immature, he was emotionally ignorant.

Joseph reported to his father some of the bad things his brothers were doing.[7]

I'm sorry, but if you're still a tattletale at seventeen, you've got EQ issues. And evidently it ran in the family. His father, Jacob, wasn't exactly an emotional Mensa member either. The entire family was emotionally dysfunctional because Jacob played favorites with his children. And one act of favoritism—giving Joseph a coat of many colors—ripped his family apart.[8]

One day Joseph dreamed that his brothers would bow down to him, and he was so self-absorbed that he thought his brothers would actually appreciate his dream. Not so much. Joseph must have missed class the day they talked about "inside thoughts." He should have kept this dream to himself, but he couldn't keep his mouth shut. He told his brothers that they would one day bow down to him. Jealousy turned into such intense hatred that his brothers faked his death and sold him into slavery. Joseph landed in Egypt and went to work for one of Pharaoh's chief officers, Potiphar. Then things went from bad to worse. False accusations of conduct unbecoming landed him in an Egyptian dungeon.

Have you ever noticed the way suffering helps us become less self-absorbed? A little suffering can produce a lot of compassion. And that is what happened to Joseph. God turned a dungeon into a classroom where Joseph learned some lessons in empathy and sympathy. He got an education in emotional intelligence.

COUNTERFACTUAL THEORY

> *While they were in prison, Pharaoh's cup-bearer and baker each had a dream one night, and each dream had its own meaning. When Joseph saw them the next morning, he noticed that they both looked upset. "Why do you look so worried today?" he asked them.*[9]

Did you catch it? Joseph *"noticed that they both looked upset."*

He noticed that they looked upset—so what? Well, it may not seem like much at first glance, but that one instance of emotional intelligence saved two nations from extinction.

Let me explain. Noticing a worried look speaks volumes about how much Joseph had matured emotionally. Joseph had enough problems of his own, right? If I'm in prison for crimes I didn't commit, I'm going to be feeling sorry for myself. I don't have the time or the energy to care about anybody else. But Joseph had developed an acute emotional sensitivity to the people around him. It's hard to believe this is the same person who couldn't read his brothers' body language when his life depended on it. But more than a decade later, he is so tuned in to the emotional states of those around him that he notices discreet facial expressions revealing an ounce of anxiety. Why? Because he's now on the far side of suffering and injustice and pain. And Joseph doesn't just discern the subtle emotional clue; he experiences a sympathy breakthrough. He is compassionate enough to get involved.

What was behind the upset look of the cupbearer was a strange dream. And when the cupbearer shared his dream, Joseph interpreted it. Three days later, the dream came true when the cupbearer was released from prison and reinstated in his office. Initially, the cupbearer forgot all about Joseph. But several years later, when Pharaoh had a strange dream that none of the Egyptian magicians could interpret, the cupbearer remembered Joseph. At the cupbearer's suggestion, Joseph was summoned to interpret the dream. He not only interpreted Pharaoh's dream, he landed a job in Pharaoh's administration.

A single act of compassion in an Egyptian dungeon years before led to a supernatural synchronicity, which led to the salvation of two nations. How? Well, Joseph was appointed chief of staff by Pharaoh. During the seven years of plenty that he himself had predicted, Joseph stockpiled enough grain to sustain Egypt through seven years of famine. But he didn't just save Egypt, he also saved Israel. During the famine, his father and brothers found safe haven in Egypt. And it was in Egypt that the family of Jacob turned into the nation of Israel.

One of my favorite branches of history is counterfactual theory. It asks the *what if* questions. What if Joseph hadn't noticed the cupbearer's upset look? Well, he wouldn't have had the opportunity to interpret the cupbearer's dream. And what if he hadn't interpreted the dream? The cupbearer would not have known Joseph could do that. And without that relational link, Joseph would never have met Pharaoh. Joseph would have died in that dungeon. Egypt would not have survived the famine. And Joseph's family, the nation of Israel, would have starved to death in Canaan. End of story. But that *isn't* the end of the story, because Joseph *did* notice that upset look. And his act of compassion toward a fellow inmate did more than save his life. It did more than save two nations. It led to your salvation and mine. Hundreds of years later, a descendant of Joseph's brother Judah was born in a small village called Bethlehem. And it was His primal act of compassion at Calvary that led to our salvation.

Never underestimate a single act of compassion, no matter how small. It can change the course of history in ways that only eternity will tell.

FIVE BUCKS

I recently gave a devotional talk for some World Vision staff. Their DC office is located just a few blocks from Ebenezers, our church's coffeehouse on Capitol Hill. Over the years, I've had a number of friends who have worked in World Vision's domestic and field offices, so I am familiar with and have tremendous respect for their organization. Roughly a hundred million people in about a hundred countries receive physical, social, and spiritual support from World Vision every year. But here is what really challenges me and inspires me: it all started with five dollars of compassion.

In 1950, the founder of World Vision, Bob Pierce, was in Korea. He felt helpless as he watched children orphaned by the Korean War standing in endless food lines. One day one of those little children dropped dead because there wasn't any food at the front of the line. It broke Bob's heart. He experienced a sympathy breakthrough. And his decision to do something about it became the defining moment of his life.

I suppose Bob Pierce could have walked away from that food line that day and forgotten all about it. That is what most of us do when we read about tragedies in the morning newspaper or watch them on the nightly news. The last thing that crosses most of our minds is actually doing something about it. Most of us let what we cannot do keep us from doing what we can. Not Bob Pierce. He made a resolution: "We're going to get food to the front of the food lines. If it kills me, we're going to do it." Getting food to the front of the line became his God-ordained passion. Bob flew back and forth between the United States and Korea, raising awareness and raising funds.

Then, on one of those trips, Bob met a little girl named White Jade, who had been beaten and disowned because of her decision to follow

Christ. All Bob had in his pocket was five bucks, and he gave it to her. But that's not all he did. He also pledged to send her money every month. That Spirit-prompted act of compassion became the catalyst for what would become World Vision's child sponsorship program.[10]

Let me ask you a question: what will kill you if you don't do it?

What makes you glad or sad or mad? What puts a holy smile on your face? What causes your spirit to sob uncontrollably? What makes you pound your fist on the table out of righteous indignation? Somewhere in the mixture of that gladness, sadness, and madness is your God-ordained passion. Or maybe I should say *compassion,* because you are feeling what God feels. And once you identify it, doing something about it isn't optional. You can't *not* do something about it.

IF THE SHOE FITS

I recently spoke at a leadership conference, and one of the other speakers was Blake Mycoskie. Blake is the chief shoe giver at TOMS Shoes. And he graciously gave every speaker at the event a pair of TOMS shoes. I love the shoes. But here's what I love even more: I love the fact that when you buy a pair of TOMS shoes, you are giving a pair of shoes to a child in a third-world country. For every pair of shoes purchased, a pair of shoes is given away.

Their mission is simple: one for one.[11]

In 2006, Blake was touring Argentina when he noticed that many of the kids didn't have shoes. He could have gone back to the United States and gone about his business. Instead, he started a business with a mission of putting shoes on the feet of those children. He returned to Argentina later that year with ten thousand pairs of shoes. Their projected shoe drops this year? More than three hundred thousand pairs of shoes.

Blake identified a need. He personalized it. Then he decided to do something about it. It didn't start out as something big. It started out as something small. But that is how primal movements begin. Someone decides to do something about something that makes him glad or sad or mad. For Blake, it was barefoot children who broke his heart. And he literally put shoes on his faith.

I have no idea what makes you glad or sad or mad. But I do know this: if each of us simply took ownership of our unique, God-ordained passions, we'd start a coup de compassion the likes of which has not been seen since the first century.

There is a Bob Pierce reading this book. I know it. There is a Blake Mycoskie reading this book. I'm sure of it. There is a God-ordained passion that makes you glad, sad, or mad. There is something that breaks your heart because it breaks the heart of God. The only question that remains is this: what are you going to do about it?

3

A Drop in the Bucket

It is more noble to give yourself completely to one individual than to labor diligently for the salvation of the masses.

—DAG HAMMARSKJÖLD

A few years ago, researchers at Carnegie Mellon University devised a study to discover how and why people respond to the needs of others. Participants were given five one-dollar bills for completing a random survey on technology products, but that survey was simply to ensure that all the participants had cash on hand to consider donating to charity. After completing the survey, participants were given an envelope with a charity request letter from Save the Children. The researchers tested two versions of the request letter. The first version featured statistics about the magnitude of the problems facing children in Africa. The other letter shared the needs of one seven-year-old girl named Rokia. On average, the participants who read the statistical letter contributed $1.14. The people who read about Rokia gave $2.38, or more than twice as much.[1]

The smaller donations in response to the statistical letter were the result of something psychologists call the *drop-in-the-bucket effect.* If we feel overwhelmed by the scale of the problem, we often do little about it. Statistics about massive human suffering in Africa can actually make people less charitable. The reason? Researchers theorized that focusing on statistics short-circuits a compassionate response by shifting people into an analytical frame of mind. And when people think analytically, it can hinder their ability to act compassionately. The head gets in the way of the heart.

The researchers wanted to validate their findings, so they devised another test. One group was primed to think analytically with questions like this: "If an object travels at five feet per minute, then by your calculations, how many feet will it travel in 360 seconds?" The other group was primed to think in terms of feelings with questions such as this one: "Please write down one word to describe how you feel when you hear the word *baby*." The results? After reading the Rokia letter, the analytically primed group gave $1.26 on average. The emotionally primed group gave $2.34. Researchers came to this conclusion: the mere act of calculation reduces compassion.

Sometimes our minds interfere with our hearts. Logical objections get in the way of compassionate actions. *It's not my responsibility. I'm not ready. I can't make much of a difference anyway.* I'm certainly not suggesting that you shouldn't count the cost. You should. But if God is speaking to your heart, don't let your mind get in the way of what God wants you to do. Sometimes loving God with all your heart simply means listening to your heart instead of your head.

The Americanized Gospel

What does it mean to love God with all our hearts?

It means our hearts break for the things that break the heart of God. It means we have identified the God-ordained passion that makes us glad, sad, or mad. It means inaction is not an option, because the compassion of Christ is the driving motivation of our lives.

Now it's time to descend a little further down that flight of stairs that leads to primal compassion. I want to go underground, below your actions to your motivations. And I want to touch on a truth that might touch a nerve ending. Honestly, I hope it makes you feel as uncomfortable as I felt when I stood in those ancient catacombs where our spiritual ancestors risked their lives to worship God.

Where your treasure is, there your heart will be also.[2]

I think it's easy to talk about things like faith and obedience and compassion in abstract terms. The more abstract, the less convicting the truth is. So let me get concrete. Faith equals God-ordained risks in the face of fear. Obedience equals God-honoring decisions in the face of temptation. And compassion equals Spirit-prompted generosity in the face of greed.

If you really want to know how I'm doing spiritually, all you need to do is look at my checkbook. It doesn't lie. It reveals my priorities. It reveals my passions. And it doesn't just reveal how I'm doing financially; it reveals how I'm doing spiritually. It's one of the best barometers of spiritual maturity I know of. Don't get me wrong. I'm certainly not reducing compassion to a financial transaction. I think generosity has as much to do with time and energy as it does with money. But sometimes love is measured in dollars.

Jesus identified an indivisible link between the heart and money. And here's what it comes down to: you can give without loving, but you cannot love without giving. And the more you love, the more you give. It's not complicated. If you want a heart for missions, for example, then give to missions. If you want a bigger heart, give more.

The American church needs a heart check. Or maybe I should say, a bank check. It seems to me that we have spiritualized the American Dream or materialized the gospel. Take your pick. And any attempt to monetize a relationship with God cheapens the gospel. Do I believe God wants to prosper His children? The answer is an unequivocal yes. But prosperity isn't measured in dollars. In fact, material prosperity has nothing to do with spiritual maturity. If it did, Donald Trump would be a saint and Mother Teresa would be a sinner. The problem with the prosperity gospel is that anytime you put an adjective in front of the gospel, you distort the gospel. The prosperity gospel has confused the ends and the means. Financial blessing is seen as an end in itself.

God doesn't want to bless you so you can drive an expensive car. Join the Junky Car Club.[3] Seriously. It's a club started by my friend Mike Foster. The mission is simple: spend less on the vehicle you drive so you can give more money to kingdom causes you care about. I'm a lifetime member. It used to be by default. I didn't have the money to buy an expensive car. Now it's a conscientious decision.

The blessings of God are never ends in themselves. And if we use a blessing selfishly, the blessing actually turns into a curse. The blessings of God are always a means to an end. And the end is blessing others. We are blessed to bless.

One of the turning points of my life came the day I stopped setting income goals and started setting giving goals. It was a paradigm shift. I finally came to terms with the fact that making money is the way you make a living and giving it away is the way you make a life. True joy is found on the giving end of life. Does that mean I don't struggle with greed? Nope. Greed is a nine-headed monster. And it has nine lives. Does that mean I don't want to make more money? Nope. It simply means that on my good days I live to give. My motivation to make more is so I can give more. John Wesley may have said it best: "Gain all you can, save all you can, give all you can."

SENIOR PARTNER

I have a ninety-three-year-old friend. Actually, he's more than a friend. Stanley Tam is one of my heroes. Gravity has certainly taken its toll on

Stanley's body. Ninety-three trips around the sun will do that. But Stanley is the youngest oldest person I know. He's almost the most generous person I've ever met.

More than half a century ago, he made a decision that would change the trajectory of his life. Stanley Tam made God his Senior Partner. At the time, the United States Plastic Corporation had an annual revenue of less than two hundred thousand dollars, but Stanley believed God would bless his business and he wanted to honor God from the get-go. So Stanley legally transferred 51 percent of his business to God. Fifty-one percent of the company's profits were set aside for kingdom causes. I'm guessing most of us would have been patting ourselves on the back at that point. Not Stanley. Stanley felt convicted. After reading the parable about the merchant who found the pearl of great price and sold everything he had to obtain it, Stanley made a decision to divest himself of all his shares. On January 15, 1955, every share of stock was transferred to his Senior Partner and Stanley became a salaried employee of the company he had started. Since the day Stanley made that defining decision, he has given away more than a hundred million dollars. But let me be clear about one thing. Stanley hasn't just given God thousands of shares or millions of dollars. What he's really given God is his heart. And that's what God really wants.

Stanley recently spoke at National Community Church. He cleared his ninety-three-year-old throat a record number of times. And his soft-spoken words were occasionally barely audible. But the decibel level of his life is ear piercing. I thought of the words of Ralph Waldo Emerson: "Who you are speaks so loudly I cannot hear what you're saying." Stanley is a brilliant communicator who has shared his story more than seven thousand times, but his life is so much louder than his words. Listening to Stanley speak was like hearing stereophonic truth.

The dinner we shared that weekend ranks as one of the most memorable meals of my life. I ate up every word that came out of his mouth. A lot of the people who meet Stanley want his money. I want his faith. Such childlike faith in such an aged body is a rare quality. He talked about good old-fashioned obedience as the key to success. He talked about giving things away as a means of sending them ahead to heaven. He talked about how God's shovel is bigger than ours. But the most challenging and inspiring discussion revolved around establishing an income ceiling. Most people spend more money as they make more money. Their standard of living goes up in direct proportion to their income. They buy more cars, bigger televisions, and nicer things. Not Stanley. He hasn't taken a raise in three decades. In his own words, "A man can eat only one meal at a time, wear only one suit of clothes at a time, drive only one car at a time. All this I have. Isn't that enough?"

That is *the* $64,000 question, isn't it?

How much is enough?

Industrialist and philanthropist John D. Rockefeller's infamous answer to that question was, "One more dollar." We have an insatiable appetite for more. But there is a way to master your money instead of letting money master you. Here's the secret: establish an income ceiling. Enough will never be enough unless you determine how much is enough. So let me ask the question: how much is enough?

Please don't just continue reading this book. Answer the question.

How much is enough?

I know it's an uncomfortable question, especially considering the fact that 1.3 billion people live on less than a dollar per day. But what would happen if every Christ follower had the courage to ask and answer that question with biblical integrity? What would happen if every Christ follower personalized that question and specified a dollar amount? What would happen if every Christ follower gave away everything above and beyond their predetermined income ceiling?

I'll tell you exactly what would happen: it would spark a primal movement the likes of which the world has not seen since the first century. Why? Because we'd be following the radical example the first Christians set:

Selling their possessions and goods, they gave to anyone as he had need.[4]

THE FOCUSING ILLUSION

Have you ever noticed that you can be perfectly content with everything you have, but one trip to the mall can ruin all of that? All of a sudden, the clothes in your closet aren't quite as cool, your décor is out of style, and your new gadgets seem old. I call it the Mall Effect. Malls are designed to feed greed. What happens is this: you focus on everything you don't have, and it produces feelings of want. Of course, the antidote is one trip to a third-world country. Seeing what others do not have will help you appreciate what you do have. You'll have a newfound gratitude for the things you take for granted. I call it the Mission Trip Effect.

A few years ago, a study that consisted of two questions was done with college students:

1. How happy are you?
2. How many dates did you have in the last month?

The researchers found a weak correlation between the level of happiness and the number of dates. But then the researchers flipped the order of the questions:

1. How many dates did you have in the last month?
2. How happy are you?

All of sudden, there was a strong correlation. What happened? The sequence of the questions forced students to focus on their dating status.

And focusing on how few dates they'd had sabotaged their general level of happiness. Psychologists call it the *focusing illusion*.

What is your financial focus?

Are you focused on what you have or what you don't have? That is the difference between gratitude and greed. Are you focused on this life or the next? That is the difference between stinginess and generosity. Are you focused on your wants or others' needs? That is the difference between selfishness and compassion. It's also the difference between unhappiness and joy.

As your focus changes, your perspective will change. As your perspective changes, your life will change. You might find yourself in the same circumstances. But your heart will change, and along with it, your motivations and expectations.

The bottom line is this: your focus determines your reality. If you focus on your wants, enough will never be enough. And your heart will get smaller and smaller. If you focus on the needs of others, you'll discover that you have more than enough. If you focus on the here and now, you'll try to hang on to everything you have. But if you focus on eternity, you'll give away everything you've got.

I love the way author Gary Thomas put it.

> *Thinking about eternity helps us retrieve [perspective]. I'm reminded of this every year when I figure my taxes. During the year, I rejoice at the paychecks and extra income, and sometimes I flinch when I write out the tithe and offering. I do my best to be a joyful giver, but I confess it is not always easy, especially when there are other perceived needs and wants.*
>
> *At the end of the year, however, all of that changes. As I'm figuring my tax liability, I wince at every source of income and rejoice with every tithe and offering check—more income means more tax,*

but every offering and tithe means less tax. Everything is turned
upside down, or perhaps, more appropriately, right side up.
       I suspect Judgment Day will be like that.[5]

I suspect he's right.

PRE-DECISIONS

The most important decisions you make are pre-decisions. Pre-decisions
are the decisions you make before you have to make the decision. And
they help you make the right decision when you have to make a tough
decision. If you don't make pre-decisions, you'll end up making lots of bad
decisions because you'll cave in to your circumstances instead of sticking
to your convictions.

When Lora and I got married, one of the pre-decisions we made as
a couple was that we would never *not* tithe. We lived off Lora's salary
while I was in graduate school. And it wasn't easy on the checkbook or the
stomach. Two words: *ramen noodles.* But from that day forward, we have
given God the first 10 percent of our income.

We don't tithe because 10 percent belongs to God. The truth is that
100 percent belongs to Him. He just lets us keep 90 percent. For the
record, God doesn't need your money. But He does want your heart. And
your heart ends up wherever your treasure ends up.

Here is a personal conviction I've come to after nearly two decades
of tithing: God can do more with 90 percent than I can do with 100 percent. If I don't tithe, I'm taking God out of the equation of my finances.
If I do tithe, I'm adding God into the equation of my finances. And He
is the God who is able to feed five thousand people with five loaves and
two fish. And have more leftover than He started with. In God's economy,
$5 + 2 = 5{,}000$ R12.[6]

Think of the tithe as an income ceiling. It's a way of saying 90 percent is enough. And honestly, it is the only antidote to greed that I know of. Why? Because it reminds you of whose money it is. And it keeps you focused on giving instead of getting. Having said that, let me say this: The tithe isn't the goal. It's the starting place. It begins with a pre-decision to live off 90 percent, but it doesn't stop there. The more we grow up spiritually, the more we'll give back to God financially. It's that simple. Why? Because you aren't giving Him your money. You're giving Him your heart.

I've always been inspired by J. C. Penney. Not the store, but the person, though he is the one who started the store. As a young businessman, he made the decision to give 10 percent of his income and live off 90 percent. By the end of his life, he was giving 90 percent and living off 10 percent.[7]

Inspiring, isn't it? But it starts with a pre-decision.

ABUNDANCE MENTALITY

One of the defining moments in the history of National Community Church was the decision to start giving to missions. I believe that God's hand of blessing on NCC is a by-product of that pre-decision to never not tithe to missions. At the time, our average attendance was thirty-five people, and their total monthly giving was two thousand dollars. We were renting a DC public school for sixteen hundred dollars a month, which left four hundred dollars for my salary and all other expenses. It was the worst of times. It was the best of times. I wouldn't trade the lessons learned during those early days for anything. It helps me appreciate every penny of God's provision now. And it was during that season that a biblical promise became one of our core convictions as a church: you cannot outgive God.

It was during the lowest-giving month in NCC history that I sensed the Lord speaking to me, but I didn't really want to hear what I thought He was saying. Ever been there? I felt like God wanted us to start giving to missions, but it didn't make sense because we weren't a self-supporting church at the time. I tried to excuse it: *How can we support others when we need support ourselves?* And I fought it for a while, but you cannot win an argument with God. If you win, you lose. And if you lose, you win. God won the argument, and I'm so glad He did. I'll never forget that first fifty-dollar check written to our first missionary. It seemed like so much money at the time. And it was money we didn't have. But like love, faith is sometimes measured in dollars. We stepped out in financial faith, and God honored it. We experienced a 300 percent increase in giving the next month, and we've never looked back.

I honestly believe that God will bless National Community Church in proportion to two things: how much money we give to missions, and how we care for the poor in our city. As long as we are doing those two things, I'm confident that God will continue to bless us beyond our ability to contain it.

A few years ago, NCC helped launch Beza International Church in Addis Ababa, Ethiopia. The kindred spirit between the two churches is difficult to put into words. Beza is NCC East, and NCC is Beza West. When I spoke at the inaugural service in 2006, there were only a handful of people, but they had a whole lot of faith. A few years and a few thousand people later, that ministry is multiplying at a first-century rate. That God-ordained dream is becoming reality so quickly that it's almost like watching a time-lapse video. And the vision continues to expand. A few months ago, we sent a team of thirty-nine NCCers to help establish a new ministry center to an AIDS colony on Entoto Mountain, a few kilometers outside the city.

Every time I visit Ethiopia, I want to give every penny I have. But that desire to give became even more defined after my last visit. An offhand comment turned into a defining moment. As he took the offering, Pastor Zeb Mengistu jokingly remarked about someone writing a million-dollar check. Everybody laughed. I didn't. The Holy Spirit quickened in my spirit what Zeb said. I actually cried. And I prayed, "Lord, let it be us." I believe the day will come when we give a million dollars to advance God's kingdom in Ethiopia.

As I flew home, I had plenty of time to reflect on the trip and dream about the future. It was somewhere over the Atlantic Ocean that God solidified something in my spirit. I have huge dreams for DC. NCC is impacting thousands of people now, but we need to be impacting tens of thousands. We currently have five locations, but there are thirty-nine movie theaters in the DC area waiting for a church to be launched. And I believe our one coffeehouse on Capitol Hill will become a chain of coffeehouses that gives every penny of its profit to missions. As long as there is one person in the metro DC area who does not have a relationship with Christ, God is not done growing His church. But let me share the driving motivation: we need to grow more so we can give more. We've come a long way since that first fifty-dollar check. In fact, our congregation will go on ten missions trips and give more than five hundred thousand dollars to missions this year. But we need to grow more so we can give more.

I think it's easy for us to operate out of a scarcity mentality: *the more I give, the less I'll have.* But it's not true. In the kingdom of God, it's the opposite. The less you give, the less you have, and the more you give, the more you have. If you hang on to what you have, your heart will become smaller and smaller. And you'll lose your soul in the process.[8] But if you give what you've got, your heart will grow larger and larger for the things of God.

That abundance mentality traces back to a biblical promise in Luke 6:38:

Give, and it will be given to you. A good measure, pressed down,
shaken together and running over, will be poured into your lap.
For with the measure you use, it will be measured to you.

When you give beyond your ability, God is going to bless you beyond your ability. It's the inviolable law of measures: you always get back more than you give away. Don't get me wrong. God is not a slot machine. If you give to get, you don't get it. And God won't honor it. But if you give for the right reasons, then you'll discover that you cannot outgive God. It's not possible. In fact, if you start giving beyond your means, you may discover that you have more left over than what you started with. That is what happens when we add God to the equation of our finances.

There are moments when loving God with all your heart won't make financial sense. But those are the moments when you need to give hilariously, ridiculously, generously, and sacrificially. It won't add up. But God will multiply it.

MULTIPLICATION ANOINTING

In the fall of 2006 I was speaking at a men's conference. It was one week before my first book, *In a Pit with a Lion on a Snowy Day*, was set to release. And one of the other speakers was Tommy Barnett. Tommy shared the story of God's provision for the LA Dream Center that he and his son, Matthew Barnett, started.[9] It was one of the most inspiring and energetic talks I've ever heard. And afterward he invited anyone who wanted a multiplication anointing to come to the altar. I'll be honest, I wasn't even sure if the idea of a multiplication anointing was in the Bible. But if Tommy was offering, I was taking.[10] It felt a little awkward going to the altar. It always does. But I wanted God's blessing on my first book.

I knew that 95 percent of books don't sell five thousand copies. But as I stood at that altar, I prayed for a multiplication anointing. I specifically asked God to multiply the book and let it sell twenty-five thousand copies. Of course, I threw in the obligatory "if it be Your will" at the end. And that sounds spiritual. But that tag line was less a submission to God's will and more a spiritual cop-out in case it didn't happen. The truth is that my whisper number was one hundred thousand copies. In the deep recesses of my heart, that is what I hoped for. I just didn't have enough faith to verbalize that number. I felt foolish enough verbalizing twenty-five thousand.

Since that book's release, God has multiplied its impact beyond what I imagined. In typical God fashion, He has exceeded my human expectations. But here's the rest of the story. I honestly believe God has blessed that book because of a financial decision we made before we even signed a contract with a publisher.

In the summer of 2005, Lora and I made the largest faith promise of our lives. A faith promise is an amount of money pledged to missions above and beyond the tithe. It's not based on a budget. It's based on faith. Honestly, we had no idea how we'd be able to give the amount of money we pledged. We knew it would take some supernatural provision. But I knew that God was going to honor it. Here's what I blogged on July 31, 2005, the day we made that pledge: "I have a confidence and anticipation that I can't even put into words. I can't wait to see how God provides what we promised."

It was two months later, on October 4, 2005, that I landed my first book contract. The advance on that four-book deal more than covered our faith promise. And writing that check, the largest check we'd ever written for a kingdom cause, was one of the greatest joys of my life. I honestly believe that that contract was God's provision. I was absolutely thrilled at the prospect of becoming a published author, but that thrill tends to fade during final edits. The thrill of giving never goes away. Compound interest for eternity.

I don't know your financial situation. But I do know this: God wants to bless you. He wants to bless you thirty-, sixty-, one hundredfold. And if you are willing to *subtract* what you are spending on yourself and *add* it to what you are investing in the kingdom, God will do the *multiplication.* Do you believe that? If you do, you'll give generously. And your heart will get bigger. If you don't, you won't and it won't.

HOPE, COFFEE & MELODY

Not long ago we hosted the Robbie Seay Band at National Community Church. On this particular tour—Hope, Coffee & Melody—they partnered with Compassion International, so after singing, they gave our congregation an opportunity to sponsor a child. Thirty-two dollars a month provides food, education, health care, and most importantly, hope! As I stood there singing, I felt like the Spirit of God asked me a question: *"Do you think I'd rather hear you sing songs or help these kids?"* It broke me. I started crying as I was singing.

Let me ask you: What do you think brings more joy to the heart of our heavenly Father—singing songs or caring for the poor? Which one is a better definition of what it really means to love God with all your heart? Which one is the greater act of worship? I hope the answer is obvious.

What if, instead of sound quality or lyrical creativity, our litmus test for worship was a heart that breaks for the things that break the heart of God? What if we saw compassion as a form of worship? Worship without words. Worship beyond words.

I felt so convicted that morning, in part, because helping a child would cost less than my DirecTV package. I have nothing against

DirecTV. The NFL Sunday Ticket is one of the luxuries I afford myself. It's the way I unwind after nine weekend services. But we live in a country that desperately needs perspective. Americans are not immune to economic recession. And this prodding is not directed to those who have lost a job or lost a home. But come on, friends, half of the world's population lives on less than two dollars per day. Less than two dollars. Maybe it's time for a reality check.

Long story short, our family decided to sponsor a little girl named Vivian in Honduras. We found out that when you sponsor a child online, you can choose a particular birthday.[11] So my daughter, Summer, suggested, "Why don't we choose a child with Grandpa's birthday?" Summer's grandpa, Bob Schmidgall, had the biggest heart for missions of anyone I've ever known. When he died more than a decade ago, the church he pastored was giving millions of dollars to missions every year. And the generosity of the church was a reflection of his heart. Sponsoring a child who shared his birthday was one small way we could continue to carry on the legacy he left to us. And more importantly, it was one way we could worship God with more than sung words.

We recently got a letter from Vivian that Lora read during our family devotions. Her simple thank-you in broken English was beyond precious. And it came with a crayon drawing that landed on our refrigerator door. The joy we experienced reading that letter was the rare kind of joy that is the by-product of compassion. It is the kind of joy that floods your heart when you've given to someone something that has made a difference in her life. It is the kind of joy that can only be experienced on the giving end of life.

When it comes to getting, it seems like enough is never enough. And the same is true with giving. It seems like enough is never enough, so we don't give anything. Let me challenge that subconscious lie that we buy into. You'll never have enough. You'll never be enough. You'll never do enough. But don't let that keep you from giving what you have, being who you are, and doing what you can. If you make a difference in the life of one little girl, isn't that enough?

The Talmud, the Jewish commentary on the Old Testament, says it this way: "Whoever destroys one life, it is as though he has destroyed a whole world; and whoever saves one life, it is as though he has saved a whole world."[12]

Don't let what you cannot do keep you from doing what you can. Put your money where your heart is. It's not a drop in the bucket. Every act of generosity creates a righteous ripple effect that can change the course of history. It will also change your heart.

PART 2

THE SOUL
OF CHRISTIANITY

4

The Island of the Colorblind

There are only two ways to live your life. One is as if nothing is a miracle. The other is as if everything is.

—ALBERT EINSTEIN

When I need a little extra inspiration, I find a corner at the National Gallery of Art to read or write or think. It's one of the perks of living a few blocks from the National Mall. The most famous collection in the gallery is the Italian Renaissance collection, which includes the only Leonardo da Vinci painting in the Americas. I'm actually sitting on a couch facing the *Ginevra de' Benci* as I write this.

If you like people-watching, the National Gallery of Art is Fenway Park. And the time spent at each exhibit is the box score. Some visitors give the da Vinci painting little more than a passing glance. Others stand before it like they are standing just outside the pearly gates and getting their first glimpse of heaven. Those who pause long enough to ponder the painting notice the artistic nuances that made da Vinci the quintessential Renaissance artist: the detailed texture, the lighting angles, the color contours. Some visitors take time to read the caption beneath the painting and learn that Ginevra was a lady of the aristocratic class living in fifteenth-century Florence. And the serious tourists taking the audio tour discover that da Vinci produced the painting on the occasion of her marriage to Luigi Niccolini. That may be the most significant revelation, given that there isn't the slightest hint of a smile on her face. Not exactly a beaming bride-to-be.

Every visitor who passes through Gallery 6 can say they've seen the *Ginevra de' Benci,* but some of them have seen it only with their eyes. Others have seen it with their soul. Some have simply given it a glance. Others have hallowed it.

Life is like that, isn't it? Some people live deeply, live fully. Their circumstances are no different than anyone else's. They breathe the same air. But they have the uncanny ability to see more, experience more, enjoy more. Others, not so much. Some people almost seem like they are half awake or half aware or half alive. They see less, experience less, enjoy less.

Leonardo da Vinci himself once observed that the average person "looks without seeing, listens without hearing, touches without feeling, eats without tasting, inhales without awareness of odor or fragrance, and talks without thinking."

As I sit on this couch observing everyone from schoolchildren to art aficionados walking by the *Ginevra de' Benci,* several thoughts cross my mind. First of all, poor Leonardo would roll over in his grave if he knew how prophetic his words were about his own painting. So many people look without seeing. But my overarching feeling is one of pity. I feel bad for those who are in such a hurry that they don't fully appreciate the beauty that is right before their eyes.

I wonder if that is how God feels.

The very first revelation of God in Genesis is that of an Artist. And the very first reaction recorded is *His* reaction to *His* creation. Like an artist at the unveiling of his own masterpiece, God steps back at the end of each creation day to look at what He has made. His reaction?

God saw that it was good.

That simple refrain is repeated each day until the sixth day. Then God steps way back to survey the full scope of creation.

God saw all that he had made, and it was very good.[1]

God is awed by His own creation. Amazing, isn't it? His primal reaction is wonderment at His own work. It's almost as if God says, "I outdid Myself, if I say so Myself."

Is anything more natural than unadulterated awe in response to the Creator and His creation? Is any emotion more primal than wonder? It is the Creator's righteous reaction to His own creation, and maybe that is why we feel so spiritual when we watch an ocean sunrise or summit a mountain or stand in the shadow of a giant sequoia. Our reaction is a godly reaction. We are doing exactly what God was doing in the beginning.

But we are doing more than that. What we are really doing is loving God with our soul. And that is something our generation desperately needs to rediscover. When we lose our sense of wonder, what we really lose is our soul. Our lack of wonder is really a lack of love.

Is it possible that we've given God a passing glance instead of truly hallowing His name? Is it possible we've settled for a god who fits into the constraints of our logical left brains instead of the God who is able to do immeasurably more than all we can imagine[2] with our right brains? Is it possible we've studied the God of logic without truly worshiping the God of wonders?

When you descend the flight of stairs into the soul of Christianity, what you discover is primal wonder. When you get past all the traditions and institutions, all the liturgies and methodologies, all the creeds and canons, what you're left with is raw wonder that is beyond logic and beyond words. It cannot be reduced to the logical constraints of the left brain. It cannot be reduced to the twenty-six letters of the English alphabet.

Wonder defies logic. Wonder defies words. And anything else or anything less is religion.

If loving God with all our heart means a heart that breaks for the things that break the heart of God, then loving God with all our soul means a soul full of wonder, a soul flooded with the glory of God, a soul awed by beauty and mystery, a soul that hallows God above all else.

AWED SILENCE

One of my prized possessions is a cheap T-shirt that says "I hiked the Grand Canyon rim to rim." That is precisely what my son Parker and I did this past summer. We hiked down the 14.2-mile North Kaibab Trail and back up the 9.3-mile Bright Angel Trail. And we did it in 110-degree heat no less. And that was in the shade! I actually dropped thirteen pounds in two days. Trust me, there are safer and easier ways to lose weight.

Reaching the south rim of the canyon was one of the greatest moments of my life. I was absolutely exhausted as we looked back at the winding trail we had just traversed, but the view was absolutely exhilarating. To celebrate our accomplishment, Parker and I checked another life goal off our list by taking a helicopter ride over the canyon. Maybe it was the physical exhaustion from the climb that contributed to my already-heightened emotional state. Or maybe it was the timing of the music, "Beautiful Day" by U2, in our helicopter headphones. But as we flew out over the canyon, I cried.

I know the word *awesome* is overused. But that is the only word that begins to capture what I was feeling as we hovered over one of the seven natural wonders of the world. Almost like an overloaded circuit that blows a fuse, I didn't have the emotional capacity to handle the current. My only outlet? Tears of worship. It was my primal reaction to the wonder I was witnessing.

One of the great mistakes we've made in modern Christianity is approaching God *deductively* as an object of knowledge instead of approaching Him *inductively* as the cause of wonder. So apologists try to prove that God is factual. And He is. But facts don't awe us. In my humble opinion, it takes far more faith to believe in macroevolution by random chance than creation by intelligent design. But it's about more than just arguing the evidence. God is more than factual. He is wonderful. The mind is educated with facts, but the soul is educated with beauty and mystery. And the curriculum is creation.

One of the unforgettable moments on our Grand Canyon adventure was the first sunrise on the first morning. It was the most spectacular sunrise I've ever witnessed. We hiked out to Bright Angel Point and climbed to the highest elevation possible—8,158 feet, according to the U.S. Geological Survey. Then we sat in awed silence as rays of light illuminated the Crayola colors of the canyon. It was like ultraviolet light revealing the Creator's fingerprints.

The more of God's creation I experience, the more I am convinced of this: awed silence in the presence of divine beauty is a form of worship that is often deeper and truer than sung words. I can't wait till my glorified eardrums can hear angels sing and my glorified vocal cords can praise God in perfect pitch. But even on the other side of the space-time continuum, our singing will be preceded and superseded by silence. Thirty minutes of it, to be exact.[3] That thirty minutes of silence in heaven, referenced in the book of Revelation, has stymied scholars for centuries. But I wonder if it's nothing more than our primal reaction to His supernatural beauty. Our first face-to-face encounter with God will leave us speechless. We'll need thirty minutes of awed silence just to catch our collective breath as we stand before the beauty of His majesty.

We need those moments of silence on this side of the space-time continuum too. It's one way we nurture a sense of wonder. Blaise Pascal, the seventeenth-century French philosopher, went so far as to say, "All of man's miseries derive from not being able to sit quietly in a room alone." Silence is one of the soul's love languages.

When we are filled with wonder, it is a foreshadowing of what we'll experience in heaven. But it's also a primal reminder that what we call *natural phenomena* are really supernatural phenomena. And we ought to celebrate them as such. The sunrise is so consistent that we take it for granted, but few things are as miraculous as the celestial dance that takes place on a daily basis. Our planet spins around its axis at a speed of 1,000 mph. And while our planet does a 360 every twenty-four hours, it is also hurtling through space at an unimaginable speed of 67,000 mph. You may not have any big plans for today, but you will travel 1.6 million miles in your annual lap around the sun. Quite an accomplishment! And to top it off, the Milky Way galaxy is spinning at approximately 490,000 mph. It takes the Milky Way two hundred million years to make one full revolution.

Almost makes you dizzy, doesn't it? Wonder will do that.

ODE TO A THUNDERSTORM

Thomas Carlyle, the nineteenth-century Scottish essayist, once said, "Worship is transcendent wonder. Wonder for which there is no limit or measure; that is worship."

In its most primal form, worship is wonder. It is standing in awe of the Creator and His creation. It is translating the beauty of creation into praise for the Creator. It is thanking God for majestic sunrises and brilliant stars and beautiful snowflakes. It is giving credit where credit is due: the Creator.

Have you ever noticed how often David refers to natural phenomena in Psalms? He praises God with broad brushstrokes: "The world's a huge stockpile of GOD-wonders."[4] But he also captures unique phenomena in distinctive detail.

Psalm 29 could be captioned "Ode to a Thunderstorm."[5]

Bravo, GOD, bravo!
* Gods and all angels shout, "Encore!"*
In awe before the glory,
* in awe before God's visible power....*

GOD's thunder tympanic,
GOD's thunder symphonic.

GOD's thunder smashes cedars,
GOD topples the northern cedars....

GOD's thunder spits fire.
GOD thunders, the wilderness quakes;
He makes the desert of Kadesh shake.

GOD's thunder sets the oak trees dancing
A wild dance, whirling; the pelting rain strips their branches.
We fall to our knees—we call out, "Glory!"[6]

Nikola Tesla was one of history's most prodigious inventors. Tesla was granted more than a hundred U.S. patents. His most famous—for alternating current—is the power system that supplies our homes with easy access to electrical power via outlets. Every time you flip a switch, you owe Tesla a thank-you.

Tesla had an idiosyncratic personality, but one ritual in particular is both revealing and inspiring. During thunderstorms, he would sit on a couch near a window in his home. Every time lightning struck and thunder clapped, Tesla would rise to his feet and applaud God. It was one genius, lowercase *g*, giving a standing ovation to another Genius, capital *G*.

For the record, there are approximately two thousand thunderstorms somewhere on planet Earth at any given time. And there are approximately one hundred lightning strikes per second, or 8.64 million lightning strikes per day! That is a lot of standing ovations. But according to the psalmist, the angels shout, "Encore!" after each one.

When was the last time you cried or clapped for the Creator? When was the last time you gave Him a standing ovation? When was the last time you thanked God for a baby's smile or a child's laugh or a spouse's touch? When was the last time you were so awed by the night sky or autumn leaves or snowcapped mountains or ocean waves that you worshiped the Creator in wide-eyed wonder like a little child?

EPIPHANY

You never know how or when or where an epiphany will occur, but at any given moment God can invade the reality of your life and give you a glimpse of His glory. And it is those unexplainable and unforgettable epiphanies that make life worth living.

I'll never forget boating to the Blue Grotto on Capri Island off the coast of Italy. The brilliant blue waters were breathtaking, and to top it off, the very Italian captain of our four-person rowboat serenaded us with a rousing rendition of *"O Sole Mio."*

I'll never forget my first safari at Awash National Park in Africa's Rift Valley. The heat of the African sun was offset by a cool wind in our faces as we sat on top of Land Rovers, praising God for every wild animal we encountered.

And I'll never forget holding our first child for the first time. Or our second. Or our third.

Have you ever had an epiphany? A moment when heaven seemed to invade earth? A moment when eternity seemed to invade time? A moment when the presence of God was so tangible that it almost felt like a cool breeze on a hot day?

One of my first epiphanies occurred when I was six years old. I can still feel the crisp December air and hear the crunch of freshly fallen snow under my grandfather's feet. We were on our way to cut down a Christmas tree, and my grandfather was holding me in his all-encompassing arms. He looked up into the Minnesota sky on that cloudless night and quoted what I now know to be Psalm 19:1: "The heavens declare the glory of God; the skies proclaim the work of his hands."

If you looked at my bookshelves, you might think I minored in astrophysics. And I often wonder if my fascination with science traces back to this genesis moment when I was six years old. I had sung "Twinkle, Twinkle, Little Star" a thousand times, but I had never really wondered what they are. I've spent an inordinate amount of time looking at the stars since then, and it is time well spent. I can't quantify this, but staring at the stars is good for your soul. It's a primal spiritual practice that is as ancient as Abraham. And as our wonder grows, so does our soul. In fact, it's our capacity for wonder that determines the size of our soul.

Thank God for epiphanies. Thank God for those moments in time that transcend time. Thank God for those moments when we discover something deeper, something truer, something greater than physical reality. Thank God for those moments when our spiritual eyes are opened to behold beauties and realities we were blind to before.

COLORBLIND

In *The Island of the Colorblind,* Oliver Sacks writes a colorful account about a tiny island in the South Pacific. Pingelap is an atoll of three small islets whose total area is less than three square miles, and the highest elevation on the island complex is only ten feet above sea level. In 1775, Typhoon Lengkieki swept over the island, destroying all the vegetation and killing 90 percent of its inhabitants. The twenty survivors resorted to fishing as the only means of survival until the island revegetated.[7]

After the great typhoon, a genetic peculiarity evolved. A surprisingly large proportion of the next generation was born colorblind. Elsewhere in the world, fewer than one in thirty thousand people is colorblind. On the island of Pingelap, one in twelve is born with the condition. The high percentage can be traced to the fact that several people in the surviving gene pool carried a rare gene responsible for congenital achromatopsia.[8]

Those of us with normal color vision have approximately seven million cones, allowing us to distinguish up to ten million different colors. Congenital achromatopes have no functional cones. They rely exclusively on the hundred twenty million low-light photoreceptor rods in the retina. As a result, they are hypersensitive to light. They often wear several pairs of sunglasses or avoid light altogether. Their poor visual acuity forces them to use a monocle—a handheld magnifying glass that looks like a telescope—to read text or see things at a distance. And, of course, they cannot perceive color.

The sad irony is that few places on earth are more beautiful or colorful than this tropical paradise. "It was striking how green everything was in Pingelap," notes Sacks, "not only the foliage of trees, but their fruits as well—breadfruit and pandanus are both green, as were many varieties of bananas on the island." The island is full of "brightly colored red and yellow fruits—papaya, mango, guava."[9] The island is literally bursting with tropical colors, but the colorblind Pingelapians cannot perceive them. They lack the perceptual capacity simply because they have no cones.

Sad, isn't it? But many of us are as blind to wonder as the Pingelapians are to color. There are miracles all around us all the time, but we lack the perceptual capacity to perceive them. We are in the presence of God, but we are unaware of it. We are surrounded by the glory of God but can't see it.

Elizabeth Barrett Browning put it in poetic terms.

> *Earth's crammed with heaven,*
> *And every common bush afire with God:*
> *But only he who sees, takes off his shoes,*
> *The rest sit round it, and pluck blackberries.*[10]

THE MIRACLE OF SIGHT

> *Ears that hear and eyes that see—*
> *the LORD has made them both.*[11]

Verses like this go in one ear and out the other. Pun intended. But it would take a lifetime to exegete and appreciate all the optical and auditory nuances of just that one verse. Ophthalmologists and audiologists have devoted entire lifetimes to studying the visual and auditory cortexes, but those processes remain a mystery. I was preaching on this passage a few years ago, and a physician in our congregation sent me this e-mail:

> *The wonder of the human body was one of the main reasons I*
> *entered the field of medicine at age twenty-one. I recently completed*
> *eight years of medical training and now have the privilege to care for*

some of the most important people in the country at the Pentagon. Honestly, each year of my medical education, my faith grew stronger and stronger simply because I was able to catch a glimpse of the amazing handiwork of God through my coursework. I also saw fellow students discover God in medical school largely as a result of their training. I sometimes wish every atheist could take Gross Anatomy or Physiology at a medical school level.

I will be honest, medical school is more about describing things in the human body, not explaining them. For example, even today we don't understand how your ear and auditory system function as an information processor, analyzer, and pattern recognizer, all from a set of chemical events set off from a few vibrations hitting your eardrum! Next time you recognize Martin Sheen's voice in a commercial or IMAX film, make sure to appreciate it!

Embryology itself is nothing but describing how a fetus develops over time. Little is known about how it occurs or how certain sets of cells know how to become a heart, how to form an eye, and how to form an ear, let alone wind up in the right spot. Yes, we understand the genetics, but not the specific reasons behind the process.

Anyway, I am just very privileged to have been able to study medicine but really also study theology at the same time. This may also explain why, when I ask patients if I can pray for them, this often means a lot more to them than anything else I could ever give them. I think deep down they know the wonder they walk around in too!

Most of us take our eyesight for granted, but even the simplest of processes is divinely complex. The retina, for example, conducts close to ten billion calculations every second, and that is before an image even travels through the optic nerve to the visual cortex.

To simulate 10 milliseconds of the complete processing of even a single nerve cell from the retina would require the solution of about 500 simultaneous non-linear differential equations one hundred times and would take at least several minutes of processing time on a Cray supercomputer. Keeping in mind that there are more than 10 million or more such cells interacting with each other in complex ways it would take a minimum of a hundred years of Cray time to simulate what takes place in your eye many times every second.[12]

Honestly, I have no idea what that even means! But that is precisely my point. It's nothing short of miraculous and mysterious. And that is the tip of the cortex. There are a thousand processes like that happening all the time. Trillions of chemical reactions are taking place in every cell every second. Your body is inhaling oxygen, metabolizing energy, maintaining equilibrium, producing hormones, repairing tissues, purifying toxins, digesting food, exhaling carbon dioxide, and circulating blood. As you read, millions of electrical impulses are firing across billions of synaptic pathways, and you don't even give it a second thought. And as important and as integral as those processes are to our survival, most of us are totally unaware of what our bodies are doing most of the time. We are far too complex to comprehend.

SIXTH SENSE

Each of our five senses is nothing short of miraculous.

The human nose can detect one-millionth of one milligram of garlic floating in the air and distinguish among ten thousand distinct odors. The hairs blanketing your body magnify the sensation of touch so that you can discern a thousandth of an ounce of pressure on the tip of a half-inch hair. Amazing, isn't it? But our five senses also come with sensory limitations. The eardrum can only hear sound waves that vibrate between 20 and 20,000 hertz. Anything outside that range is inaudible. The human eye can only perceive light waves that are between 0.00007 and 0.00004 centimeters long. Anything outside that range is invisible.

Let me try to put our visual limitation in perspective. Our visual range is the equivalent of one playing card in a stack of cards stretching halfway across the universe. In other words, we see a very thin slice of reality. And the same is true spiritually. I think of omniscience as a complete 360-degree perspective, logically and chronologically. God sees all the way around everything. He sees everything from every angle because He exists outside our space-time dimensions. Our perspective, on the other hand, is very limited, logically and chronologically. The most brilliant among us have less than one googolplex of 1 percent of perspective. And that ought to keep us humble.

Some things cannot be perceived. They can only be conceived.

Some things cannot be deduced. They can only be imagined.

Some things cannot be learned. They can only be revealed.

"No eye has seen,
*   no ear has heard,*
no mind has conceived
*   what God has prepared for those who love him"—*
but God has revealed it to us by his Spirit.[13]

The Holy Spirit compensates for our sensory limits by enabling us to conceive of things we cannot perceive with our five senses. Think of Him as a sixth sense. The revelation of the Spirit gives us extrasensory perception. He helps us see the invisible and hear the inaudible. But that sixth sense has to be cultivated much like our five senses.

When babies make their grand entrance into the world, their visual resolution is one-fortieth of that of a normal adult. They lack depth perception. And their visual range is only about thirteen inches. The world is low-definition, two-dimensional, and only thirteen inches in diameter. Slowly yet sovereignly, the world begins to take on width and breadth and depth. By four months, a baby can perceive stereoscopic depth. By six months, visual acuity has improved fivefold, their black-and-white world has burst into a kaleidoscope of colors, and they have volitional control of their eye movements. And by his or her first birthday, the child sees the world almost as well as an adult.

Our eye for wonder develops in much the same way. Before our spiritual eyes are opened, the world is only thirteen inches in diameter. It's like we live in a low-definition, two-dimensional world. Then the Holy Spirit gives us depth perception. He opens our eyes to see the ordinary miracles that surround us, the ordinary miracles that are us. It's like spiritual cataracts are removed to reveal a reality that was always there. Slowly yet sovereignly, the soul takes on width and breadth and depth as it is filled with wonder. It expands to the size of our God-given imagination and beyond.

PERCEPTUAL VIGILANCE

I recently read a fascinating study involving a group of Americans who had never been to Mexico and a group of Mexicans who had never been to America. The researchers built a binocular viewing machine capable of showing one image to the right eye and one image to the left eye. One of the snapshots was of a baseball game, a traditional American pastime. The other photo was of a bullfight, a traditional Mexican pastime. During the test, the pictures appeared simultaneously, forcing subjects to focus on one or the other. When asked what they had seen, the American subjects reported seeing a baseball game, while their Mexican counterparts reported seeing a bullfight.[14]

On one level, seeing is believing. But the opposite is true as well: believing is seeing. Our perceptions are greatly affected by experiences, education, and expectations. The psychological term is *perceptual vigilance*. What we see largely depends upon what we have experienced or have not experienced, what we know or don't know, what we expect or don't expect. That is why Americans see a baseball game while Mexicans see a bullfight.

Now let me take it a step further: we generally see what we want to see and don't see what we don't want to see. If you don't believe me, just observe two die-hard fans of opposing NFL teams watching the same instant replay. How can one fan be so sure the receiver was out of bounds while the other fan is sure the receiver had possession with two feet inbounds? The answer is simple: We see what we're looking for. Or to put it another way, if we aren't looking for it, we won't see it. That is why naturalists miss the miracles that are all around them all the time. They don't have a cognitive category for the supernatural, so they explain away what they cannot explain.

Shortly after moving to Washington DC, I took Lora to a performance of the National Symphony Orchestra at the Kennedy Center. Honestly, I don't even remember what the orchestra was playing. All I remember is the guy next to me. I almost went deaf in my left ear. When I go to a football game, I expect some crazed fans, but at the symphony? This guy got up out of his seat and gave the conductor a standing ovation the moment he stepped on stage. I could barely stay awake, while Mr. Symphony was on the edge of his seat yelling, "Bravo!" I thought they only did that in the movies. His hands had to be black and blue the next day from all his clapping. This thought kept going through my mind all evening: *Are we listening to the same orchestra?*

At the end of the evening I came to this conclusion: either Mr. Symphony needed to get a life, or he had a deep appreciation for music that put me to shame. I wanted to think it was the former, but I'm guessing it was the latter.

Remember the old adage? Beauty is in the eye of the beholder. Everything is, isn't it? The emotions we experience don't reflect external reality; they reflect internal reality. We don't see the world as it is; we see the world as we are. So wonder, or the lack thereof, simply reveals what is in our souls. If our souls are full of wonder, then life is wonderful. Why? Because you see with your soul. And when you see with your soul, everything becomes a reflection of the glory of God.

> *Your eyes are windows into your body. If you open your eyes wide in wonder and belief, your body fills up with light. If you live squinty-eyed in greed and distrust, your body is a dank cellar. If you pull the blinds on your windows, what a dark life you will have!*[15]

SLEEPWALKING

My youngest son, Josiah, is a sleepwalker. At first, his glassy-eyed look spooked us. So did the wild and wacky stuff he said and did. He seemed to be wide awake because his eyes were wide open, but eventually it was his sleep talking that gave away the fact that he was sleepwalking. Josiah has a great sense of humor when he's awake, but he turns into a stand-up comic when he's sleepwalking. He says some of the most incoherent yet most hilarious things!

For what it's worth, I've had only one sleepwalking episode that I'm aware of. I was ten years old at the time, and it wasn't a very long walk. I got out of bed, went down the hall, walked into my brother's room, and opened his middle dresser drawer. I won't tell you what happened next, but my parents walked in just in time to see me trying to flush the dresser.

Somnambulism is a curious sleep disorder. Episodes usually take place during the third or fourth stage of the sleep cycle. Sleepwalkers engage in normal activities as if they are awake. Their eyes are wide open, but they are unawake and unaware of their surroundings. And after an episode, they have no recollection of what happened.

I wonder how many of us suffer from some sort of spiritual somnambulism. Our eyes are open, but the vacant look reveals an empty soul. At best we're half awake. And just like the physical condition, we're unaware of our spiritual condition until someone or something wakes us up. We're unaware of the miracles happening all around us all the time. We're unaware of the spiritual warfare that is being waged all around us all the time. We're unaware of what the Spirit of God is doing all around us all the time.

Jacob was a spiritual sleepwalker. Ironically, the thing that woke him up to the spiritual realities surrounding him was a deep-sleep REM cycle. Jacob went to sleep in and woke up in the same place, but he went to sleep and woke up a different person.

> *He had a dream in which he saw a stairway resting on the earth,*
> *with its top reaching to heaven, and the angels of God were ascending*
> *and descending on it....*
>
> *When Jacob awoke from his sleep, he thought, "Surely the LORD*
> *is in this place, and I was not aware of it." He was afraid and said,*
> *"How awesome is this place! This is none other than the house of*
> *God; this is the gate of heaven."*[16]

A few years ago our family vacationed in Frisco, Colorado. We flew into Denver on a night flight, so it was already pitch black outside as we made the drive through the Rocky Mountains. It was my first time in Colorado, and I wasn't sure what to expect. I definitely noticed the mountain shadows, but I couldn't make out any of the defining features. We managed to find the condo, unpack our luggage, and collapse into bed.

I'll never forget waking up the next morning. It was a sneak peek of what it will be like to go to sleep on earth for the last time and wake up in heaven for the first time. It was like we went to sleep one place and woke up someplace totally different, but the only thing that changed was our perspective. Light revealed what had been there all along. I looked out the kitchen window and saw the majestic mountainscape. It was like looking at the lyrics of "America the Beautiful." I was surrounded by purple mountain majesties.

I wonder if that was what it was like for Jacob. Jacob went to sleep in Luz, but he woke up in Bethel. His circumstances had not changed, but his perspective would never be same. Nothing had changed, but everything had changed. Jacob didn't just wake up physically, he woke up spiritually. Until that epiphany, Jacob had been living with his eyes wide shut. After this wake-up call, he saw God everyplace he looked. He finally noticed the God who had been there all along. And his soul was filled with wonder.

You never know where or when or how God will invade your life, but He can show up anywhere, anytime, any way. And that ought to fill us with holy anticipation. God can show up at any moment and change everything. Of course, the great irony is that it often happens when we least expect it.

GOD-CONSCIOUS

Several years ago we were having a dinner party at our house when Parker came running through the family room yelling, "Captain Underpants!" Sure enough, all he had on was underpants. Adults don't do that. Why?

Because we're self-conscious. But kids don't care. Psychological innocence is the sacred right of childhood. But eventually and unfortunately, most of us become so tangled up in our own self-consciousness that we have a hard time experiencing the joy of just being ourselves. On a theological note, I think negative self-consciousness is part of the Curse. It wasn't until Adam and Eve ate from the tree of the knowledge of good and evil that they became conscious of their nakedness. Wonder was displaced by shame.

Sooner or later, children lose their Edenic innocence and become self-conscious. Give it a few more years and they enter another stage of consciousness. They notice the opposite sex, and opposites attract. And once you wake up to that reality, there is no turning back. When I first started liking Lora, it was almost like I had radar that alerted me every time she was around. I was acutely aware of her presence. Everything I did, I did with a consciousness of her presence. I tried to look a little cooler and talk a little smoother when she was around, not always with the intended effect.

So there is a moment when we become self-conscious. There is a moment when we become conscious of the opposite sex. In a similar sense, there is a moment when we become God conscious. For some, it's something beautiful that forces us to find Someone to thank. For others, it's something tragic that forces us to find Someone to help. But somehow, someway, we become aware of the God of Jacob who was there all the time. We have a Bethel experience. And thus begins our spiritual journey.

> *Your life is a journey you must travel with a deep consciousness of God.*[17]

God consciousness is the most primal form of consciousness. And the longer we journey, the more aware of His presence we become, until we see Him everywhere all the time. Spiritual maturity has nothing to do with circumstances. It has everything to do with consciousness. A relationship with Christ doesn't always change our circumstances, but it does change the way we see ourselves, see others, and see God. Why? Because we see with our souls. We become less self-conscious and more God-conscious. It's almost like a second childhood. As we recapture a childlike sense of wonder, we perceive everyone and everything for what it really is: a miracle.

It was G. K. Chesterton who once stated that he learned more about life from observing children at play in a nursery than he ever learned from the books in his library. He also observed that the older one gets, the more it takes to fill the soul with wonder. Ultimately, only God is big enough to do that. And He's big enough to do it for eternity.

5

Seventy Faces

The words printed on the pages of my Bible give witness
to the living and active revelation of the God of creation
and salvation, the God of love who became the Word
made flesh in Jesus, and I had better not forget it. If in my
Bible reading I lose touch with this livingness, if I fail to
listen to this living Jesus, submit to this sovereignty, and
respond to this love, I become arrogant in my knowing
and impersonal in my behavior. An enormous amount of
damage is done in the name of Christian living by bad
Bible reading. *Caveat lector,* let the reader beware.

—Eugene Peterson

In 1801, Sir David Brewster was awarded an honorary master of arts
degree from the University of Edinburgh and was ordained to preach.
But his first sermon turned into his last sermon. Brewster was so nervous
when he got behind the pulpit that he vowed to never do it again. In the
words of a colleague, "It was a pity for the National Church of Scotland,
but a good day for science." Brewster decided to pursue his first love, the
science of optics. And in 1816, his childlike passion produced an invention that has captured the imagination of children ever since. Brewster
called it a kaleidoscope. Containing fragments of colored glass at the end
of a mirrored tube, the kaleidoscope reflects light in an endless variety of
colors and patterns.

And so it is with Scripture.

According to rabbinic tradition, every word of sacred Scripture has seventy faces and six hundred thousand meanings.[1]

If I had to describe Scripture in a single word, it would be *kaleidoscopic*. You can read the same verse on different occasions and it will speak to you in totally different ways. It reminds me of the adage attributed to the Greek philosopher Heraclitus: "You never step into the same river twice." In a similar vein, you never read the same verse of Scripture the same way twice. And that is a testament to its divine Author. The Spirit who inspired the writers of Scripture thousands of years ago is the same Spirit who illuminates readers today. And His illumination of Scripture is based on His intimate and infinite knowledge of your personality, your circumstances, your dreams, your doubts, your history, and your destiny. That is why Scripture speaks to us in such kaleidoscopic ways.

The Bible was written over a span of fifteen hundred years by more than forty writers. God inspired kings and poets and prophets and shepherds. They wrote out of very different personalities in very different circumstances. Some wrote in the plush setting of a palace, while others etched their words during an island exile. Some wrote out of the agony of personal tragedy, while others wrote in the ecstasy of an epiphany. Written in three different languages on three different continents, there is no other book like the Bible. Despite the fact that it touches on thousands of complex subjects and controversial topics, it possesses a supernatural harmony from beginning to end. And it is omnirelevant to every person on the planet.

When we open the sacred Scriptures, it is like descending that flight of stairs at the Church of San Clemente and walking into the catacombs of truth. The Bible is the place where God bares His soul. And it's no Sunday school flannelgraph. It'll make you wince and cringe and blush. But it'll also make you marvel. Nothing speaks to the soul like Scripture.

It's the way God reveals His wonders in written form. And like the wonders of creation waiting to be discovered, the Bible beckons us to explore.

The quest for the lost soul of Christianity always leads us back to the Bible. But rediscovering the wonders of Scripture requires more than reading. That's where the quest begins, but that's not where it ends. Not if you want to get it into your soul. You have to meditate on it. Then you have to live it out. Meditating on it turns one-dimensional knowledge into two-dimensional understanding. Living it out turns two-dimensional understanding into three-dimensional obedience.

FREQUENCY

Right now you are surrounded by countless radio waves. You cannot see them or hear them or feel them. But if you tune a radio to AM 980, you'll pick up radio waves transmitting at 980,000 hertz. And as long as you're on that wavelength, a world of information is opened up to you.

Not unlike the radio waves that transmit voices and pictures and signals at different frequencies, the Spirit of God is always broadcasting.[2] But we've got to tune in to His frequency. The Holy Spirit has multiple channels of communication. He speaks through His creation. He speaks in a still, small voice. He speaks through sanctified desires, divine appointments, and open doors. He speaks through Spirit-prompted friends who care enough to rebuke, correct, and exhort. And thank God for all those frequencies. But His primary channel of communication is Scripture. When we open the Bible, it's like God opens His mouth. That's how we get on His frequency. That's how we tune in to His voice.

He who has ears, let him hear.[3]

I recently read about a musical trainer hired to work with opera singers who could not hit certain notes within a particular octave even though the notes fell within their vocal range. It was a musical mystery. The trainer did extensive testing on their vocal cords, but he couldn't find any reason why they couldn't hit those notes. Then, on a whim, he tested their hearing. And what he discovered is that these opera singers could not sing a note they could not hear. The problem wasn't singing. The problem was hearing.

Until you hear the voice of God, you won't be able to sing His song. Why? Because you're out of tune. That's how we get stuck in sinful habits and negative cycles and destructive patterns. But when you open the Bible and really hear the voice of God—His loving voice, His graceful voice, His powerful voice, His convicting voice, His affirming voice, His authoritative voice—your life begins to echo God's. Your life becomes a joyful noise. Your life begins to harmonize with the Holy Spirit.

For a brief stint during our dating days, Lora and I attended different colleges. Ultimately, I transferred from the University of Chicago to Central Bible College because the phone bills cost more than tuition. It was cheaper to transfer! We spent hours on the phone. Why? Because the sound of her voice sent tingles down my spine.

When you love someone, you love the sound of his or her voice. If you've ever had a long-distance relationship, you know whereof I write. A relationship with God is a lot like that. To love God is to love His voice. Or to put it another way, to love God is to love His Word.

COVER TO COVER

We all go through seasons when God seems silent. We seek a word from the Lord and He doesn't seem to answer. At least not how or when we want. I was in one of those places last year. I couldn't seem to hear God above the white noise of my life. All I could hear was static. And the primary reason, in retrospect, was because I wasn't reading the Bible nearly as much as I could have or should have. This is embarrassing to admit, but for me Bible reading had become synonymous with sermon prep. I was reading it professionally instead of devotionally. I was reading it for what God wanted to say *through me* instead of what God wanted to say *to me*. And my soul suffered because of it.

Then I stumbled across an interview with renowned author and theologian J. I. Packer. And one particular statement rang true: "Any Christian worth his salt ought to read the Bible from cover-to-cover every year." I felt convicted by it, and I couldn't argue with it. It made sense, so much sense that I decided to do it. And it's the best decision I've made this year. I've fallen in love with the Bible all over again.

Because I have a goal-oriented personality, I knew I needed to turn this spiritual discipline of Scripture reading into a spiritual goal, so I made one New Year's resolution: read through a one-year Bible. For what it's worth, I chose *The Daily Message*. And in case you care, I'm thinking about going old school and reading through the King James Version next year just to mix it up. After making the resolution myself, I then recruited my son Parker to do it with me. Honestly, I had ulterior motives. I knew that if my son was doing it with me, it would help to keep *me* accountable!

Do I ever miss a day? Yes. Is it always easy? No.

There are days when reading through a book like Leviticus feels like driving through Nebraska. No offense, Nebraskans, but long stretches of flat land can be mind numbing. Truth be told, some parts of the Bible are more exciting than others. Is that okay to say? All Scripture is equally inspired, but not all Scripture is equally applicable.[4] So if you're bored with the Bible, here's my advice: keep reading. You'll eventually get out of Nebraska. And the flatlands of Nebraska will help you appreciate the scenic overlooks in Colorado almost like reading about the blood and guts of animal sacrifice under the Old Covenant helps you appreciate the once-and-for-all sacrifice that Christ made on the cross.

Spiritual disciplines are a lot like physical disciplines. I don't always feel like working out, but I always feel better for having done so. It takes some determination to maintain the discipline. But it's the daily disciplines that will ultimately determine our destiny. And if you maintain the discipline long enough, the discipline will turn into a desire. Start reading the Bible and you'll discover that the more you read, the more you crave. It's an acquired taste.

One of the common complaints people make when leaving a church is this: "I'm not being fed." As a preacher, I make it my goal to nourish our congregation via a well-rounded diet of sermons. And I try to preach every sermon like it's my last. But let me push back a little. My kids learned to feed themselves when they were toddlers. If you're not being fed, that's your fault. I'm afraid we've unintentionally fostered a subtle form of spiritual codependency in our churches. It is easy to let others take responsibility for what should be our responsibility. So we let our pastors study the Bible for us. Here's a news flash: the Bible was unchained from the pulpit nearly five hundred years ago during an era of history called the Middle Ages.

If you are relying on a preacher to be fed, I fear for you. Listening to a sermon is acquiring secondhand knowledge. It is learning based on someone else's experiences. A sermon is no replacement for firsthand knowledge. I'd rather have people hear one word from the Lord than a thousand of my sermons. And that happens when you read the Word for yourself.

If you want to grow spiritually, you need a consistent diet of Scripture. In fact, you will never outgrow your diet of Scripture. There is no substitute. There is no supplement. "Everything we eat has some…effect upon us," observed poet T. S. Eliot. "It affects us during the process of assimilation and digestion; and I believe that exactly the same is true of anything we read."

We are what we read. But let me take it one step further. Reading without meditating is like eating without digesting. If you want to absorb the nutrients, you can't just read it; you've got to chew on it. Meditation is the way we metabolize Scripture. That's how it gets into our soul.

HINDSIGHT BIAS

The French writer Jacques Réda had a peculiar habit. He used to walk the streets of Paris with the intention of seeing one new thing each day. It was the way he renewed his love for the city. I think we renew our love for God the same way. Our love grows as we discover new dimensions of His personality, and His personality is primarily revealed in the pages of Scripture.

What if we approached Scripture the way Jacques Réda walked the streets of Paris?

I know this sounds strange, but sometimes I wish I could forget the entire Bible and start from scratch. Why? Because the Bible loses some of its shock value when you know how every story ends. Before the Israelites start marching around Jericho, we know the walls will come tumbling down. Before David picks up a stone for his slingshot, we know he will defeat Goliath. Before the wise men begin tracking the star, we know it will lead them to a little town called Bethlehem, where they will find the Messiah. Before Peter steps out of the boat, we know he's going to walk on water. And before Jesus is crucified, we know He will be resurrected on the third day.

We've read the stories so many times that we're blind to the beauty. We read with old eyes. What should shock us doesn't even faze us. What should make us gasp makes us yawn. Psychologists call it *hindsight bias*. We're inclined to see the events recorded in Scripture as more predictable than they really are. The result? We miss the drama in the Drama. I love Dorothy Sayers's assessment of the situation.

> *Official Christianity, of late years, has been having what is known as "a bad press." We are constantly assured that churches are empty because preachers insist too much upon doctrine—"dull dogma," as people call it. The fact is the precise opposite. It is the neglect of dogma that makes for dullness. The Christian faith is the most exciting drama that ever staggered the imagination of man—the dogma is the drama.*[5]

So how do we recapture the most exciting drama that ever staggered the imagination of humanity? How do we rediscover the drama in the dogma?

Here's the secret: you can't just read the Bible; you have to meditate on it. Reading gives breadth to our understanding, but meditation gives depth. If all we do is read Scripture, then our understanding is one-dimensional. Reading without meditating is like taking one glance through the kaleidoscope without turning it. So many colorful and beautiful patterns of truth remain undiscovered simply because we think we've seen everything there is to see when we haven't seen anything yet.

> *I have more insight than all my teachers,*
> *for I meditate on your statutes.*[6]

Eight times, the word *meditate* is repeated in Psalm 119. Granted, it's the longest chapter in the Bible. But still. There is a rhyme and reason to every repetition in Scripture. It's like the psalmist underlines the word eight times. Yet despite the repetition, meditation ranks as one of the most misunderstood and least practiced spiritual disciplines in our multitask culture. And it's our souls that suffer.

The word *meditation* conjures up lots of connotations. In some Eastern religions, it is the practice of emptying one's mind. But biblical meditation is the opposite. It is filling the mind with the Word of God. If the goal of reading is to get through the Bible, the goal of meditation is to get the Bible through us. Or in keeping with the metaphor, meditation is turning the kaleidoscope to reveal new patterns of light.

ALPHA WAVES

Louis Agassiz was a celebrated nineteenth-century paleontologist and Harvard professor who introduced a teaching method that discouraged textbooks and encouraged firsthand observation. And Agassiz practiced what he preached. According to Harvard legend, Agassiz once returned to the classroom after summer vacation and told his students he had spent the entire summer traveling and had only made it halfway across his backyard!

One of his students, Nathaniel Southgate Shaler, wrote in his autobiography about one of Agassiz's assignments. Agassiz pulled out a specimen jar and said, "Take this fish and look at it; when I think you're done I'll question you." After an hour or so, Shaler thought he'd observed everything there was to observe, but Agassiz didn't question Shaler that day. He didn't question him the next day. In fact, it was a week later that Agassiz said, "Tell me what you've seen." During that time, Shaler, who thought he'd seen everything there was to see, began to notice new things about the fish: the symmetry of the scales, the number of teeth, the position of the gills, the paired organs. Shaler shared his observations, but Agassiz still wasn't satisfied that Shaler had seen everything there was to see. He spent another week of ten-hour days looking at that fish from every angle imaginable. Shaler wrote in his autobiography that by the end of two weeks, he had made observations that astonished himself and satisfied Agassiz.[7]

We are too easily satisfied in our study of Scripture. Or should I say, we are too easily dissatisfied? Maybe that is why we're so infrequently astonished.

Whenever I'm reading the Bible and I get to a verse that I already understand or obey, I tend to read really slowly. I take time to pat myself on the back before turning the page. But when I get to a verse that I don't understand or don't obey, my natural tendency is to speed-read. My pace picks up because I don't like the confusion or conviction it causes. But here's a rule of thumb: when you feel like reading fast, you need to read slow. And if you do, God will reveal new patterns of truth. The truth won't just get into your short-term memory, it will get into your eternal soul. And instead of just imparting information, it will lead to transformation.

Let me put it in neurological terms.

The human brain typically produces beta waves that oscillate between thirteen and twenty-five cycles per second, but when we are in a state of relaxed alertness, the brain produces alpha waves that oscillate between eight to twelve cycles. So what? Well, some truths are only comprehended via contemplation. You quite literally have to get on the right wavelength. If surface knowledge is sufficient, beta waves will suffice. But the only way to get truth into your soul is via alpha waves. You can't just think with your mind. You have to think with your soul.

Saint Ignatius of Loyola taught his followers a spiritual exercise called *imaginative meditation.* He encouraged them to enter the gospel stories. Imagine the sights and sounds and smells. Move from the role of spectator to that of participant. Instead of reading about the crucifixion, play a role. Imagine what Mary must have felt as the man she rocked to sleep as a little baby was hanging half naked on the cross. Take the place of the thieves on either side of Jesus as they faced the same fate but for very different reasons. Play the part of Simon, who carried the cross down the Via Dolorosa. What was Barabbas, the murderer who was set free, doing while Jesus was crucified in his place? Ignatius even encouraged discussions with characters in the story, especially Jesus.

What would happen if you tried this exercise? I suggest that you do. And then meditate on how the experience impacts you. It will not only reveal something about God, it will also reveal something about yourself.

Some truths cannot be deduced by left-brain logic. They can only be induced by right-brain imagination. I realize that that may not sound scholarly enough for some, but we are far too analytical in our reading of Scripture. We dissect Scripture instead of letting Scripture dissect us. We approach it like a textbook, analyzing the words with our logical left brains. But until it captures our right-brain imagination, we'll be nothing more than half-minded, half-hearted, half-souled Christians.

Meditation is the mechanism whereby one-dimensional knowledge becomes two-dimensional understanding. But it doesn't end there. Obedience is the mechanism whereby two-dimensional understanding becomes three-dimensional faith.

STATIC STATE

A few years ago I read something rather random, but I've never forgotten it: "Dynamic properties are not revealed in the static state."[8] Too many of us try to understand truth in the static state. We want to understand it without doing anything about it, but it doesn't work that way. You want to understand it? Then obey it. Obedience will open the eyes of your understanding far more than any commentary or concordance could. I think many of us doubt Scripture simply because we haven't done it. The way you master a text isn't by studying it. The way you master a text is by submitting to it. You have to let it master you.

As I've grown spiritually, I've noticed that I speak and write less theoretically and more experientially. I'm not sharing information. I'm sharing convictions. Verse by verse, the Bible becomes more than theory. It becomes my firsthand experience.

Whatever you bind on earth will be bound in heaven.

This verse, Matthew 18:18, used to confuse me. "Whatever you bind on earth will be bound in heaven." What does that even mean? It was secondhand theory because I had no firsthand experience. Let me tell you how my confusion turned into a conviction.

Almost a decade ago I was walking by a run-down, graffiti-covered piece of property on Capitol Hill. As I walked in front of 201 F Street NE, a God idea was conceived in my spirit: *This crack house would make a great coffeehouse.* At the time, National Community Church was an upstart church plant with barely any people and even less money. It was a ridiculous idea. But I couldn't get it out of my spirit. The location was perfect: five blocks from the Capitol, one block from Union Station, and kitty-corner to a construction project that would become the largest office building in DC.

We started praying that God would give us that piece of property. Honestly, that is all we could do, because we didn't have the money to buy it. So we did prayer walks around it. We laid hands on the walls. We even trespassed on the property a few times to do prayer meetings. National Community Church now owns that property and operates the largest coffeehouse on Capitol Hill. In fact, Ebenezers is the number-one-rated coffeehouse in the metro DC area.[9] Not only do we serve hundreds of customers seven days a week, but every penny of profit goes to missions. It's coffee with a cause. And its performance space doubles as one of our five church locations, hosting two Saturday night services.

Now here's the rest of the story.

We purchased that million-dollar piece of property for $325,000, which was a miracle in and of itself. Then we discovered that four parties had offered more money than we did. And two of the bidders were real estate developers. What I'm getting at is this: we shouldn't own that piece of property. So how did we get it? My only explanation is Matthew 18:18. When we started praying for that property in the earthly realm, God put a binding contract on it in the heavenly realm.

Matthew 18:18 is more than a verse I've memorized with my mind. It's a conviction deep within my soul. Why? Because I haven't just read it, I've experienced it. I'm absolutely convinced that we underestimate our authority in Christ when we pray in alignment with the will of God. What we bind on earth is a done deal in heaven!

What I'm about to share has the potential to revolutionize the way you read the Bible. It also has the potential to revolutionize your prayer life. The Bible isn't meant to be read *re*actively. It is meant to be prayed *pro*actively. There are thousands of promises waiting to be claimed.

So many people struggle with cultivating a prayer habit simply because they don't know what to say. Their prayers consist of overused and misapplied Christian clichés. Or they feel like prayer is a one-way monologue. The truth is, the Bible is God's way of initiating a conversation with us. And it turns prayer into a dialogue. God talks to us via Scripture, then we talk back. Not only does it give you plenty to talk about, but also when you pray the Bible, you pray with more confidence because you're not just praying your words. You're praying the Word of God.

TWO TRANSLATIONS

The Bible is not an end in itself. In other words, the goal of knowing the Bible isn't Bible knowledge. The goal of knowing the Bible is knowing God. Anything less is bibliolatry. One of the great mistakes we've made in Christendom is equating spiritual maturity with knowledge acquisition, but head knowledge never has been and never will be the litmus test. The truth is that most of us are already educated way beyond the level of our obedience. We learn more and do less, thinking all the while that we're growing spiritually.

> *Do not merely listen to word, and so deceive yourselves. Do what it says. Anyone who listens to the word but does not do what it says is like a man who looks at his face in a mirror and, after looking at himself, goes away and immediately forgets what he looks like. But the man who looks intently into the perfect law that gives freedom, and continues to do this, not forgetting what he has heard, but doing it—he will be blessed in what he does.* [10]

The Latin word for "listen" is where we get our word *audit*. When you audit a class, you take in lots of information, but you don't do anything with it. You don't do the homework, or if you do, you don't turn it in to get it graded. You don't take the tests. And you don't get any credit either. The same is true in our spiritual lives. You don't get credit for auditing Scripture. You've got to put it into practice. Every word of Scripture, with its seventy faces and six hundred thousand meanings, must be translated via obedience.

In the Western world, we make a distinction between knowing and doing. But there was no such distinction in ancient Jewish thought.

Knowing was doing and doing was knowing. If you didn't do it, you didn't really know it. Knowledge isn't enough. Truth must be translated with your life.

What if, every time we came across a verse that told us to do something, we thoughtfully and prayerfully figured out a way to translate it with our lives? What if we consistently, creatively, and courageously acted on each verse? What if we turned every verse into a holy experiment?

That's what National Community Church did with Acts 1:8 this year. Our goal was to turn that verse into a verb by tithing our congregation to missions. And more than 10 percent of our congregation went on short-term trips last year. We called it our A18 Initiative.

You will receive power when the Holy Spirit comes on you; and you will be my witnesses in Jerusalem, and in all Judea and Samaria, and to the ends of the earth.[11]

In the past ten months we've taken ten missions trips to ten countries. We're building an orphanage in Uganda and a ministry center for an AIDS colony in Ethiopia. We're rescuing women from sex slavery in Thailand and building a rehab center for addicts in Trinidad and Tobago. We're reaching out to street kids in Ireland and poverty-stricken families in the Dominican Republic. Most importantly, we're proclaiming the good news of the gospel. But we're not just doing it with our words. We're doing it with our lives.

What is the best translation of Acts 1:8? It's not with your mind. It's with your life. You can read it. You can meditate on it. But it doesn't translate if you don't live it out. You can't just audit it. You have to act on it. Obedience is the way your life becomes a unique translation of the Bible. And, ultimately, it's the way you love God with all your soul.

We have access to dozens of Bible translations in every size, shape, and color imaginable. So we tend to take Scripture for granted. But I'm grateful for the men and women across the centuries who have devoted their lives to translating the sacred text into new languages. I think of the seventy-two Jewish elders recruited by Ptolemy II to translate the Old Testament from Hebrew into Greek. I think of the forty-seven scholars who translated the Textus Receptus into Elizabethan English. Some translators, such as William Tyndale, even gave their lives to give us their translations. Tyndale was burned at the stake.

The energy they invested and the sacrifices they made ought to increase our appreciation for Scripture. But my point is much loftier than that: *you* are among the company of translators. For better or for worse, your life is your unique translation. Just like the Septuagint or King James Version, your life translates Scripture into a language that those around you can read. God doesn't just want to speak *to* you through Scripture; He wants to speak *through* you. He wants to write His-story through your life. And Scripture is the script.

Read it. Meditate on it. Then live it out.

PART 3

THE MIND
OF CHRISTIANITY

6

Holy Curiosity

A mind stretched by a new idea never returns to its original shape.

—Oliver Wendell Holmes

A few years ago, Dr. Eleanor Maguire led a team of researchers in a groundbreaking study involving a group of London taxi drivers. The researchers obtained the brain scans of sixteen drivers who worked for the distinguished Black Cab Company. When comparing these drivers with non–taxi drivers in the control group, researchers noted a distinct difference in neuroanatomy. The taxi drivers had a larger hippocampus than the non–taxi drivers. More specifically, they had an enlarged posterior hippocampus, the part of the brain responsible for remembering and processing spatial information.

I was in one of those quintessential black cabs during a recent visit to London. And I certainly appreciated the elegance and convenience of my ride. What I wasn't fully cognizant of at the time was what a complicated cognitive feat it was transporting me from the rail station to Buckingham Palace. While that is certainly one of the easiest runs in London, drivers need an intimate knowledge of the six square miles surrounding Charing Cross, the transportation hub of London. After three years of training, only three-quarters of the drivers-in-training make the cut. Drivers not only need to memorize four hundred prescribed runs, but they also have to cross-reference thousands of street names, map midcourse corrections in their minds, and know how to get from any point in the city to any other point while taking into account a myriad of factors, including time of day, traffic patterns, and construction delays. And all of that is a function of a tiny seahorse-shaped component of the brain buried deep within the medial temporal lobe. Taking all of that into consideration, I probably should have given my driver a better tip, or at least complimented him on his amazing hippocampus.

During their study of the taxi drivers, the team of researchers at University College London made one other discovery that flew in the face of a longstanding assumption. For decades, the prevailing opinion had been that the brain loses its plasticity as it ages. In other words, we stop making new synaptic connections and start losing them. But researchers observed a direct correlation between the length of time spent driving a taxi and the size of the posterior hippocampus. The drivers with the longest tenure had the largest posterior hippocampus.[1] And that discovery led to this paradigm shift: neurogenesis in the posterior hippocampus persists in the adult human brain.[2]

Makes your day, doesn't it?

Let me try to translate.

God has created us with the capacity to keep learning until the day we die. And that isn't something we should take for granted. The average brain is only the size of a softball and weighs approximately three pounds, yet neurologists estimate that we have the capacity to learn something new every second of every minute of every hour of every day for the next three hundred million years. Awesome, isn't it? But it's more than that. It's also an awesome responsibility. Learning isn't a luxury; it's a stewardship issue.

It's impossible to pinpoint what percentage of our minds we use, but there is untapped potential in all of us. Your imagination is capable of far more than you imagine, if I can say it that way. Yet somewhere along the way, most of us stop living out of imagination and start living out of memory. We stop creating the future and start repeating the past. And that is the day we stop living and start dying. Why? Because we stop learning.

Loving God with all your mind means making the most of your mind by learning as much as you can about as much as you can. But the true litmus test of spiritual maturity isn't how much you know. It's knowing how much you don't know. It's coming to terms with the fact that God is not an object of knowledge as much as He is a cause of wonder. And that sanctified sense of wonder fuels a holy curiosity to keep learning more about the Creator and His creation.

> *The man who thinks he knows something does not yet know as he ought to know.*[3]

We know just enough to think we know a lot. That is our greatest problem and greatest danger, intellectually. Like teenagers who don't know how much they don't know, we're so proud of our one-dimensional knowledge of the Creator and His creation. And we're so sure of our systematic theologies that quantify and classify the Unquantifiable and Unclassifiable One. But quantifying and classifying always lead to demystifying. And when you demystify God, you're guilty of intellectual idolatry. You end up with a god, lowercase *g*, who fits into nice, neat cognitive categories. But the god who conveniently fits within the confines of your mind will never fill your soul with wonder.

There is an indivisible linkage between loving God with all your soul and loving God with all your mind. Wonder and curiosity are spiritual cousins. When the soul stops wondering, the mind stops learning. And vice versa. A lack of wonder breeds a lack of curiosity, and a lack of curiosity breeds a lack of wonder. Either way, when you stop learning, you start dying intellectually. But the spiritual implications are more profound than that. When you stop learning, you stop loving. Why? Because loving is learning more and more about the one you love. True love is never satis-fied. It always wants to know more about the object of its affection. The more you love God, the more curious you become. When it comes to loving God with all your mind, curiosity is both the cause and the effect.

MAGNUM OPUS

Nothing in all creation is more mysterious or majestic than the three pounds of gray matter housed within the human cranium. It's the mag-num opus of God's creative genius. Nuclear imaging has given our gen-eration a glimpse into the inner sanctum of the human mind. Dr. Harry Chugani, a pioneer in positron emission tomography (PET scans), likens the millions of neurons firing across trillions of synaptic pathways to a nuclear reactor. Even the simplest of processes sets off a firestorm of brain activity.

For what it's worth, a baby's brain pulsates at about 225 times the rate of the average adult's brain. Parents, that just about explains everything, doesn't it? No wonder they're bouncing off the walls. I hope that helps you exercise a little more patience the next time your kids get antsy.

On a grand scale, the brain consists of two hemispheres connected by approximately three hundred million nerve fibers called the corpus cal-losum. Think of the two hemispheres of the brain as parallel processors. They certainly overlap in function. And this is a gross simplification of something that is divinely complex, but the left brain is linear and logi-cal, while the right brain is intuitive and creative. Neurologists have also mapped regions and subregions responsible for a variety of neurological functions. The auditory cortex, for example, processes sound waves that hit the eardrum and translates them into intelligible language. The amyg-dala helps us process a vast array of emotions. The motor cortex choreo-graphs our muscle movements. And the medial ventral prefrontal cortex is the seat of humor. So whether you're humming a hit from the eighties, interpreting facial expressions, swinging a baseball bat, or solving a sudoku, a unique part of your brain is responsible for performing each of those nuanced actions.

So what does all of that have to do with the Great Commandment? You might be tempted to think the answer is *nothing*. But if we interpret the Great Commandment literally, and we should, then the answer is *everything*. Loving God with half your mind isn't good enough. Being half-minded is no better than being halfhearted. God wants to sanctify every part of your mind for His purposes: sanctified logic, sanctified intuition, sanctified imagination, even a sanctified sense of humor. The word *all* is all-inclusive.

So how do you love God with your medial ventral prefrontal cortex? You do it by cultivating that part of your mind and using it for His purposes. Humor isn't just healthy, it's holy. I'm absolutely convinced that the happiest, healthiest, and holiest people on the planet are the people who laugh at themselves the most. And that cognitive capacity is one of God's greatest gifts. God is no cosmic kill-joy. He is the one who created us with the ability to juxtapose things and find them funny.[4] It's part of the image of God. And it's one way we love God with our minds.

Honestly, I don't want a relationship with someone I can't laugh with. It would be utterly boring. And in the case of God, eternally boring. So let me ask a question: when was the last time you and God shared a good laugh? My family can attest to the fact that my prayers are often interrupted by an outburst of laughter. In fact, I can get downright slaphappy. I, for one, believe that joking can be a form of praying. I know that almost sounds sacrilegious, but I think that is because we underestimate God's sense of humor just like we underestimate His glory or His goodness. There is nothing I love more than laughing with my kids. My kids crack me up all the time, and I have only three of them. What with seven billion of us running around this planet, I wonder if God ever stops laughing. There have to be millions of hilarious things happening every moment. And the heavenly Father loves sharing a laugh with His children.

There are ways of loving God with our minds that don't often enter our minds. Humor is one of them. So is logic. So is imagination. So is consequential thinking. So is strategic planning. Even how you manage your auditory and visual cortices has more do with your spiritual health than you realize.

Loving God with all your mind literally means loving God with *all* your mind. It means managing your mind. It means making the most of your mind. It means loving God logically and creatively, seriously and humorously, intuitively and thoughtfully.

DISUSE SYNDROME

Physician and Stanford University School of Medicine professor Walter Bortz is credited with coining the term *disuse syndrome*. He originally used the phrase to describe how negligence in the area of physical activity can destroy health. Use it or lose it. That is a basic tenet of physiology. If you stop using any part of your body, including your mind, it atrophies. Like muscles that grow through exercise, the brain is capable of far greater endurance and imagination than we imagine. And when we exercise it repeatedly, it grows stronger and larger by recruiting new neuronal connections. That's why the left angular gyrus, which plays an important role in language processing, is larger in bilinguals than in monolinguals. Bilinguals use it more. But if you fail to use your mind, it atrophies. And when the mind atrophies, the soul shrivels.

I recently read that the average college graduate reads two books per year.[5] My first reaction was this: *why waste your money on an education if you're going to stop learning once you graduate?* The goal of a good education isn't learning. The goal ought to be a lifelong love of learning. And two books a year doesn't cut it. I know we're busy, but no one is too busy to go to the bathroom, right? So here's an idea. If you simply put a book in your bathroom, you can read at least one book a month.

Up until my senior year of college, I'd probably read a grand total of two dozen books not assigned by teachers. And most of them were sports biographies with lots of stats and pictures. I wasn't a reader, but that changed when I picked up an eight-hundred-page biography of Albert Einstein during a road trip with our basketball team. Somewhere along Interstate 44 between Kansas City and Springfield, Missouri, I developed a reading addiction. And it's one Einstein quote in particular that inspired me. It has become a personal mantra:

> *The important thing is not to stop questioning. Curiosity has its own reason for existence. One cannot help but be in awe when he contemplates the mysteries of eternity, of life, of the marvelous structure of reality. It is enough if one tries merely to comprehend a little of this mystery every day. Never lose a holy curiosity.*[6]

I love the juxtaposition of those two words: *holy curiosity.*

Few minds can compare to that of Albert Einstein. If ever there was a person who could be or should be considered a genius, it's Albert Einstein, isn't it? Yet Einstein himself said, "I have no special gift. I am only passionately curious."[7]

One of my graduate degrees is in education. Entire courses were devoted to teaching methodologies that lead to long-term memory retention, so it's rather ironic that I've forgotten everything but one thing. The one thing I remember is that the Latin word for "education" means "to draw out." That struck me because, if you analyzed the methodologies of most schools, including the graduate school I was attending, you would think it meant "to cram in."

Most academic programs revolve around force-feeding knowledge rather than unleashing curiosity. The result? We learn some things. But we lose what is most important: the love of learning. Curiosity dies a slow death. And we forget most of what we learned in the first place anyway. In one classic study at a top university, summa cum laude graduates were given their same final exams one month after graduation. They all failed.[8]

When you try to cram truth into the mind, it rarely gets past the short-term memory. And it definitely doesn't get into the soul. I'm afraid that that is what happens in most churches most weekends. I'm afraid we've lost our holy curiosity. We've settled for thoughtless theologies and mindless methodologies. Why? Because it's much easier to give answers than to ask questions. But Jesus didn't just give answers. Have you ever noticed how often Jesus answered a question with a question? It seems to me like we're afraid of questions. We're afraid of asking them, and we're afraid of answering them. Listen, God would much rather entertain a genuine question born out of humility than a disingenuous prayer born out of pride. We've got to keep it real with God. And we've got to keep it real with one another. If we aren't talking about the real problems, real issues, and real questions people are facing, then we are going to lose our prophetic voice.

The quest for the lost soul of Christianity is a quest driven by questions. Any question. Every question. But especially the most difficult and most important questions: *Who is God? Who am I? And what is the true purpose of life?* Holy curiosity isn't satisfied with easy answers. It doesn't settle for the platitudes we've picked up along the way. Holy curiosity asks the tough questions, the honest questions, the questions everyone else is afraid to ask. God isn't threatened by those questions. He loves them.

Like the parent of an inquisitive toddler, God sometimes laughs at our questions. But He always welcomes them.

The church ought to be the most curious place on the planet. We ought to be a safe place where people can ask dangerous questions, but all too often we're guilty of answering questions that no one is even asking. We ought to be challenging the status quo, but all too often we're guilty of defending it. But what if? What if we stopped force-feeding answers and learned to unleash the primal curiosity in our congregations?

THE GENESIS COMMISSION

Curiosity is a holy instinct. It's our curiosity regarding God that fuels an insatiable desire to know Him. It's our curiosity regarding His creation that fuels an innate drive to discover. And that holy curiosity is as old as Eden. The quest for the lost soul of Christianity takes us all the way back to the beginning of time.

> *Be fruitful and increase in number; fill the earth and subdue it. Rule over the fish of the sea and the birds of the air and over every living creature that moves on the ground.*[9]

I think it's assumed by many that Adam and Eve would have remained in the Garden of Eden forever if they had not eaten from the tree of the knowledge of good and evil, but that is a misreading of the text. Long before Adam and Eve were banished from the garden, God told them to "fill the earth and subdue it." This was humankind's first commission.

Stop and think about it. God was inviting Adam and Eve to explore. Everything outside Eden was uncharted territory. They could travel 24,759 miles in any direction and never see the same landscape twice. There were 196,949,970 square miles of virgin territory to explore. Not unlike Christopher Columbus, who was commissioned by the king and queen of Spain to find a westward route to the East Indies, and not unlike Lewis and Clark, who were commissioned by President Jefferson to explore the newly acquired Louisiana Purchase, Adam and Eve were commissioned by God to explore planet Earth. So please don't miss this primal truth: one way we glorify God is by exploring and educating ourselves about everything He has created. The innate impetus is holy curiosity. And the result is the praise of discovery.

The astronomer who charts the stars, the geneticist who maps the human genome, the researcher who seeks a cure for Parkinson's disease, the oceanographer who explores the barrier reef, the ornithologist who studies and preserves rare bird species, the physicist who tries to catch quarks, the chemist who charts molecular structures, and the theologian who studies God have one thing in common. All of them are explorers. They are fulfilling the Genesis commission. And their exploration honors God if it's done for the right reasons and results in the right response: to know Him and to worship Him.

There will always be scientists who come to atheistic conclusions. They reject the One who created their curriculum. But just because they keep faith out of the equation of science doesn't mean we should keep science out of the equation of faith. Albert Einstein said it best: "Science without religion is lame," and conversely, "religion without science is blind."

Think of it this way. The Creator designed us with two eyes, and those two eyes give us depth perception. If we had only one eye, it would be difficult to judge distances. Everything would seem flat. And we would have a difficult time putting things into perspective. That is precisely what happens when we turn a blind eye to the sciences. We lose depth perception. In my experience, a breadth of scientific knowledge deepens my faith. It adds dimensionality to my theology.

A Game of Cat and Mouse

I split my undergrad education between the University of Chicago and Central Bible College. The curriculum at CBC focused on theology, and I studied everything from pneumatology to soteriology to eschatology.[10] But if you asked me which undergraduate class had the greatest spiritual impact on my life, I would have to say it was a class on immunology at the University of Chicago Hospital Center. My professor didn't refer to God once in her lectures. I'm not even sure she believed in God. But every lecture on the immune system was like a sermon on Psalm 139:14: "I praise you because I am fearfully and wonderfully made." I remember walking out of one of those classes literally praising God for white blood cells.

That class gave me a profound appreciation for the intricacies of the immune system. But even more importantly, it conceived in me a deeply held conviction that every *-ology is* a branch of theology. Why? Because every discovery reveals a new dimension of God's creativity and personality.

If God created everything, then everything bears His sacred fingerprint. All truth is God's truth. Sure, Scripture is in a category all by itself as God's written revelation. But mathematics reveals a unique dimension of God's personality too. So does art. So does science. So does everything that reveals something about the Creator. And that is why we ought to be interested in everything.

"There is not one square inch of the entire creation," said Abraham Kuyper, "about which Jesus Christ does not cry out, 'This is mine! This belongs to me'!"

God gave Solomon wisdom and very great insight, and a breadth of understanding as measureless as the sand on the seashore.... He spoke three thousand proverbs and his songs numbered a thousand and five.

He described plant life, from the cedar of Lebanon to the hyssop that
grows out of walls. He also taught about animals and birds, reptiles
and fish. Men of all nations came to listen to Solomon's wisdom, sent
by all the kings of the world, who had heard of his wisdom.[11]

King Solomon was a Renaissance man twenty-five hundred years before the Renaissance. His knowledge wasn't confined to theology. He had extensive knowledge ranging from botany to entomology to herpetology. I like to think of Solomon as the patron saint of curiosity. Evidently he was interested in everything. And I wonder if it was his breadth of knowledge that gave him such a depth of wisdom.

It is that same King Solomon who made a fascinating statement in Proverbs:

It is the glory of God to conceal a matter;
*   to search out a matter is the glory of kings.*[12]

Francis Bacon, the sixteenth-century English writer, had a fascinating take on this proverb:

Solomon the king, although he excelled in the glory of treasure and
magnificent buildings, of shipping and navigation,…of fame and
renown, and the like, yet he maketh no claim to any of those glories,
but only to the glory of inquisition of truth; for so he saith expressly,
"The glory of God is to conceal a thing, but the glory of a king is to
find it out"; as if, according to the innocent play of children, the
Divine Majesty took delight to hide his works, to the end to have
them found out; and as if kings could not obtain a greater honour
than to be God's playfellows in that game.[13]

It is almost like God is playing a game of cat and mouse with creation. And we are His playfellows. I think God loves it when we discover something or experience something that's new to us, even if those discoveries are common knowledge. Isn't that a normal parental response when our children make new discoveries? Now, here's the exciting thing: the game never ends. Eternity won't be long enough to discover all that God is or praise Him for all that He has done.[14]

Did you know that astronomers estimate the existence of hundreds of billions of galaxies?[15] That is more than ten galaxies per person alive today! You won't run out of things to do or discover during your earthly tenure. And you certainly won't run out of things to do or discover on the other side of the space-time continuum either. Heaven will be anything but boring. It's taken thousands of years for billions of humans to explore one tiny planet in one tiny galaxy. And we've barely scratched the surface. Exploring the wonders of the new heavens and new earth will keep us curious forever. And our love for God will grow infinitely larger.

NINE DOLPHINS

I was recently listening on my iPod to a lecture delivered at a TED (Technology, Education, Design) conference.[16] Listening to TED lectures is a form of intellectual exercise I get while doing my physical exercise on an elliptical. During this particular lecture, Al Seckel, an expert in visual perception, showed the audience a wide variety of images. One of them was a stenciled drawing of a couple intimately embracing. The audience immediately recognized the image. But Seckel revealed that when that image was shown to children, almost like a Rorschach test, and they were asked to describe what they saw, the children could not see the couple. Why? Because the kids didn't have a prior memory to associate with the picture. They didn't have a cognitive category for a couple intimately embracing. Most of the kids saw nine dolphins!

Here's why: you cannot see what you do not know. Even our imaginations are limited to extrapolations of what we have seen or heard or experienced. Ideas don't materialize out of thin air, unless of course it's a God idea that bypasses the five senses and is revealed by the Holy Spirit. But by and large, our imaginations have boundaries based on our experience and education. The goal of learning is to expand our God-given imagination so we expand our appreciation of who God is and what God has made.

In his book *Mozart's Brain and the Fighter Pilot,* Richard Restak shares a profound truism: learn more, see more. He says, "The richer my knowledge of flora and fauna of the woods, the more I'll be able to see. Our perceptions take on richness and depth as a result of all the things that we learn. What the eye sees is determined by what the brain has learned."[17]

When astronomers look into the night sky, they have a greater appreciation for the constellations and stars and planets. They see more because they know more. When musicians listen to a symphony, they have a greater appreciation for the chords and melodies and instrumentation. They hear more because they know more. When sommeliers sample a wine, they have a greater appreciation for the flavor, texture, and origin. They taste more because they know more.

Simply put: the more you know, the more you appreciate.

So what? Well, how much you know may have more to do with how much you love God than you think. Consider what Jesus said to the Samaritan woman at the well: "You Samaritans know very little about the one you worship." Another translation says, "You Samaritans worship what you do not know."[18] The Samaritans were worshiping God out of a lack of knowledge. And when you worship out of ignorance, worship is empty. God doesn't just want you to worship Him; He wants you to know *why* you worship Him.

Any other husbands guilty of apologizing to your wife without really knowing what you're sorry about? You just want to end the argument. I've been guilty of this on occasion, but sometimes Lora calls my bluff. She will ask me what I'm sorry about, and I will honestly have no idea. That kind of apology is disingenuous, isn't it? If you don't even know why you're sorry, it's an empty apology. I think a lot of us worship God that way. We lip-sync words on a screen, but it's empty worship. We don't really know *why* we're worshiping Him. If God interrupted our singing and asked us why we're singing what we're singing, we'd be speechless.

God is Spirit, and his worshipers must worship in spirit and in truth.[19]

We tend to think of spiritual and intellectual pursuits as mutually exclusive endeavors, but they are anything but. Great love is born of great knowledge. In fact, your spiritual potential is a derivative of your knowledge of the Creator and His creation. Don't get me wrong—knowledge does not automatically translate into worship. If it did, university libraries would be a cacophony of praise instead of a cone of silence. But in some respects, quality of worship is determined by quantity of knowledge. The more you know, the more you have to worship. Simply put: learn more, worship more.

There should be no disconnect between spiritual and intellectual pursuits. The mind and soul are not enemies. They are allies. I don't think you can be spiritual, in the truest sense of the word, without being intellectual. And I don't think you can be intellectual, in the truest sense of the word, without being spiritual. As the mind expands, so does the soul.

If we interpret the Great Commandment mathematically, loving

God is 25 percent intellectual. In other words, love is not a mindless thing. You cannot truly love what you do not really know. That is called ignorance. So stop and think about the implications. The less you know God, the less you love Him. And the more you know God, the more you love Him. Why? Because to know Him is to love Him. And if you don't love Him, it's because you don't really know Him.

CRITICAL REALISM

In the philosophy of science, there is a concept known as *critical realism.* It is the humble acknowledgment that we don't know everything there is to know. In the words of Russell Stannard, "We can never expect at any stage to be absolutely certain that our scientific theories are correct and will never need further amendment."[20] Is it possible that the same is true of our theological theories? We not only need a degree of critical realism when it comes to science, we also need a degree of critical realism when it comes to faith.

From time to time, I offer this disclaimer to our congregation: "As soon as I'm omniscient, I'll let you know. But I wouldn't hold your breath." It's a healthy reminder for me and for them. I refuse to pretend to know more than I really know. And that humble admission frees me up to ask questions and admit doubts. In other words, it allows me to keep learning.

Why do we have such a tough time admitting our non-omniscience? Why is it so difficult to admit our deep-seated doubts? Why don't we profess what we *don't* know as readily as we explain what we do know?

I wonder if our certainties actually expose our insecurities. The more insecure we are, the more certainty we try to project, especially in the realm of theology. We're so afraid of losing our corner on the truth that we cling to our theories and theologies more tightly. Can we loosen our grip a little? I'm certainly not suggesting that we back off the core beliefs of the Christian faith. Jesus Christ is the Son of God. He lived a sinless life. He died a substitutionary death on the cross. And He was raised from the dead on the third day. Those are nonnegotiables.[21] If you remove those doctrinal cornerstones, the foundation of Christianity fails. Why? Because Jesus Christ is the Cornerstone. But there are also peripheral issues, both theological and methodological, that God-fearing, Christ-loving, Bible-believing Christians will never agree upon. It's not that they aren't important. They are. But our salvation is not contingent upon them. And that's when we need to agree to disagree in a spirit of humility.

There is an awful lot of sideways energy in the kingdom of God. We're so busy arguing with one another that we don't have any energy left over to love our neighbors. What would happen if we spent less energy defending ourselves and more energy learning from one another? Again, if something is heretical or blasphemous, we need to call it what it is. But if it's not, we'd better allow some biblical latitude. Critical realism demands it.

Our lack of omniscience simply means we don't have a 360-degree perspective. We can't see around every theological corner, which means we might have a corner on the truth, but not all four. In fact, most of us have a difficult time seeing past whatever denomination of Christianity we grew up in. That's one reason why I'm glad I grew up a denominational mutt. Our family went to half a dozen different churches when I was growing up, and here is what I learned: all of them got some things right, and all of them got some things wrong. If only I knew what they got right and what they got wrong!

In the preface to our core belief statement at National Community Church, we cite Rupertus Meldenius, a German theologian who was a voice of unity during a divisive time in church history. His four-hundred-year-old words have stood the test of time: "In essential things, unity. In nonessential things, freedom. In all things, love."

Can we quit acting as if we have God all figured out? You can know God, but to think that you can know God in the fullest sense of the word would be laughable if it weren't so detrimental. Because of the accumulation of and access to knowledge, our generation knows so much. Yet in the timeless scheme of things, we know so little. What would happen if we had the intellectual courage to admit our ignorance? I honestly think that humble confession would win more converts than our dogmatism. I'm certainly not suggesting that we don't defend the faith with intellectual integrity and confidence. But humility comes first. Humility is what wins an audience, because it is disarming and endearing.

Maybe it's time to admit that we don't know all the answers. But we know the One who does. Maybe we've been offering the wrong thing. We offer answers. God offers a relationship through Jesus Christ. His answer to our questions isn't knowledge. It's a relationship. And that relationship is the answer to every question.

DON'T TAKE YES FOR AN ANSWER

One of my inspirations is Leonardo da Vinci. Da Vinci ranks as one of the most curious and creative minds in history. Born on April 15, 1452, Leonardo dreamed of things never before imagined: a flying machine, a parachute, an extendable ladder, the bicycle, an adjustable monkey wrench, hydraulic jacks, a water-powered alarm clock, and for all of you concert lovers, the world's first revolving stage. One biographer called him "the most curious man who ever lived." But my favorite description of da Vinci? "He wouldn't take yes for an answer."[22]

I love that approach to life. If you approach every person, every challenge, every situation with humble curiosity, it transforms each of them into a learning opportunity. The outcome is no longer seen as success or failure, good or bad, positive or negative. The only measuring stick is this: what did you learn from it? Honestly, that mind-set has helped me get through some difficult challenges. When I'm going through a tough time emotionally or relationally or spiritually, I figure I'm getting an education in that area. When it gets really tough, I think of it as graduate work. Call it a Jedi mind trick. Call it a state of denial. All I know is this: That mind-set has resulted in an experimental approach to life and ministry. I'm less afraid of failing, because I know it's the best form of education. I'm less focused on getting out of situations and more focused on what I can get out of those situations. I'm less concerned with what I'm experiencing and more concerned with what I'm learning. Everyone and everything becomes part of my education. God redeems them and uses them to shape me into the person He wants me to become. And the learning process never ends.

The New Testament Greek word translated as "disciple" comes from a root that means "learner." By definition, a disciple is someone who never stops learning. A true disciple makes the most of the hundred billion brain cells God has put on loan to him. A true disciple loves more because she knows more. A true disciple is consumed with holy curiosity that doesn't take yes for an answer. The disciple keeps asking and seeking and knocking.[23] And the quest is never over because the questions never end.

Leonardo da Vinci carried a notebook with him wherever he went. It's estimated by some that da Vinci left fourteen thousand pages of notes to Francesco Melzi in his will. Nearly seven thousand pages still exist, and in case you care, Bill Gates purchased eighteen pages for $30.8 million in 1994. Da Vinci's napkin scribbles ranged from botany to anatomy to philosophy to painting. And one of the things that made them remarkable is the fact that most of them were written using a technique called *mirror writing.* He wrote in reverse so the text could be read only when reflected in a mirror. But here is what truly inspired me. In the final days leading up to his death on May 2, 1519, Leonardo apologized to God and to man "for leaving so much undone." He had done so much, but he felt like there was so much left to do. He had learned so much, but he felt like there was so much more to learn. And he was determined to keep learning until the day he died. So even on his deathbed, Leonardo was observing and describing, in scientific detail, the nature and symptoms of his illness.[24]

I know this sounds strange, but I want to die the same way. I don't want to die from the same illness. But I do want to learn something new the day I die. Why? Because I can. And because I believe that learning glorifies God when it's done for the right reasons. And that reason is to know Him more so that you can love Him more.

So go ahead and live as if you'll die tomorrow. But keep learning as if you'll live forever.

After all, you will.

One God Idea

All the forces in the world are not so powerful as an idea
whose time has come.

—VICTOR HUGO

Everything that exists was once an idea in someone's mind.[1] Before becoming a physical reality, it was nothing more than an electro-chemical signal firing across synapses deep within the cerebral cortex. The layout of the city where I live, for example, existed in the mind of a French-born architect named Pierre Charles L'Enfant long before it became a physical reality. The symmetry of the streets and the locations of government buildings were first conceived in his mind. Those ideas were then transferred to a 20-ounce piece of paper, which now sits enshrined in a 108-pound Plexiglas case breathing pressurized argon gas. It is one of five such documents on life support at the Library of Congress. And those written plans eventually became the cityscape of Washington DC via decades of manual labor, millions of dollars, and tons of physical material. When I negotiate traffic on Constitution Avenue, round Dupont Circle, or drive by 1600 Pennsylvania Avenue, I am driving down the streets L'Enfant dreamed of. My physical reality was once nothing more than an idea in the mind of Pierre Charles L'Enfant.

In a similar but infinitely grander sense, everything that exists originated in the mind of the Almighty. It was a thought before it became a thing. And that includes you. You were once an idea in the imagination of God. And for the record, God doesn't have bad ideas.

The first revelation of God in Scripture is that of a Creator. If God is anything, He is infinitely creative. Just look around you. The evidence is everywhere. I was watching Animal Planet with my kids recently, and one random fact caught my attention. Did you know that there are more than three thousand species of walking sticks? I found that astounding. But that's nothing. Entomologists have discovered and differentiated among more than three hundred fifty thousand species of beetles. That seems to border on creative overkill, but it reveals something about God's personality. God loves variety. And your fingerprint is exhibit A. There never has been and never will be anyone like you. But that isn't a testament to you. It's a testament to the God who created you.

Now let me use a little left-brain logic to make a point about right-brain creativity: if God is infinitely creative and we are not just created in His image but called to be conformed to His image, then creativity isn't optional. Creativity is a dimension of spiritual maturity. To become more like the Creator is to become more creative. When we use our sanctified imagination to serve His purposes, we are doing what God does best and loves most. And the heavenly Father takes great pride and joy in it. What parent hasn't hung a piece of kindergarten art on a refrigerator? Just as we celebrate creativity in our kids, so God celebrates creativity in us. He loves it. And it's one way we love Him.

Have you ever noticed how many times Psalms tells us to sing a new song? That creative command is repeated no fewer than half a dozen times.[2] Evidently God gets tired of old songs. He doesn't just want you to worship Him with your memory; He wants you to worship Him with your imagination. Love isn't repetitive. Love is creative. As love grows, you need new lyrics and new melodies. You need a new song to express new dimensions of love. If you tell your wife that you love her the same way over and over again, she may stop believing you at some point. Why? Because your words are an expression of memory instead of an expression of imagination. It's half-hearted because it's half-minded.

I know that most people don't classify themselves as creative, but that's because we have a narrow definition of creativity. We think of it in terms of a piece of art, a new invention, or an entrepreneurial idea. And those are certainly expressions of creativity. But that is a very thin slice. Creativity isn't just for artists or inventors or entrepreneurs; it's vital in every area of life. And the truth is that all of us are incredibly creative in certain circumstances, such as making excuses or rationalizing sin. For better or for worse, most of us are more creative than we give ourselves credit for. And using that creative potential for God's purposes is one way we can love Him.

In the broadest sense, creativity is any use of the imagination. And it becomes an act of obedience, an act of faith, and an act of love when we use it for God's glory.

HALF-FORMED IMAGINATION

I love history and I value history. The past not only puts the present into perspective, it also helps us navigate the future. That's why every Christian ought to read *Foxe's Book of Martyrs*. We ought to study classics like *The Imitation of Christ* by Thomas à Kempis and the *Confessions* of Augustine. A little church history goes a long way in giving us a broader perspective on Christianity chronologically and denominationally. Whether we recognize it or not, our present reality is a by-product of the imaginations of those who have gone before us. And if we lose our sense of history, we lose our sense of destiny.

When we forget where we come from, we forget where we're going. And memory failure certainly puts the future of the church in jeopardy.

But the greatest threat to the future of the church is a failure of our God-given imagination.

C. S. Lewis once referred to himself as the most reluctant convert in all of Christendom. The night before his conversion, he had a long conversation with fellow writer and friend J. R. R. Tolkien. Tolkien tried to convince him of the credibility of Christ, but Lewis was full of objections. Then at a critical moment in the conversation, Tolkien countered Lewis's objections with a profound statement: "Your inability to understand stems from a failure of imagination on your part."

A failure of imagination.

That isn't a peripheral problem. It's our primal problem.

Lack of faith is not a failure of logic. It's a failure of imagination. Lack of faith is the inability or unwillingness to entertain thoughts of a God who is able to do immeasurably more than all we can ask or imagine.[3] Thank God for logic. Without it, nothing would make sense. So it's not that imagination is more important than logic. It's just more neglected. A loss of curiosity has led to a loss of creativity.

In his book *The Celtic Way,* Ian Bradley writes about the celebration of imagination in the Celtic tradition. Their ancient approach to faith is a lifeline for modern minds that have lost their imaginative moorings. Bradley gets to the soul of the problem: "Too many Christians today, brought up on the penny plain prose favored by Rome and even more the Reformers, have half-formed imaginations."[4]

Half-formed imagination. That is our intellectual shortcoming. But it's more than that. It's also our spiritual shortcoming. A half-formed imagination results in a half-formed soul.

The quest for the lost soul of Christianity is about rediscovering our creative birthright. It's about reimagining everything from the Great Commandment to the Great Commission. It's about challenging old assumptions by asking the *why* questions. It's about challenging the perceived limits of our God-given potential by asking the *why not* questions. And it's driven by a holy curiosity that won't take yes for an answer.

If we are going to have an eternal impact on our culture, we can't just criticize it or copy it. We've got to create it. If we are going to reach our generation with the gospel, we can't just appeal to logic. We've got to capture their imagination. And C. S. Lewis is a great example of both. Can you think of anyone more left-brain logical than Lewis? His theological writings, from *Mere Christianity* to *The Problem of Pain,* are as logical as logic can be. But Lewis combined left-brain logic with right-brain creativity. The Chronicles of Narnia continue to capture the imagination of new generations.

THE MOST CREATIVE PLACE ON THE PLANET

The church ought to be the most creative place on the planet. And there are certainly pockets of ingenuity and imagination, but we're nowhere near our creative potential. In too many church circles, there is at best ambivalence toward creativity. And at worst there is downright animosity. We're suspicious of creativity because creativity breeds change. And change threatens the status quo. It's far easier to find something wrong with something new than to admit something is wrong with the old way of doing things. So we assume that creative churches are somehow watering down or dumbing down the gospel. And there are instances where that's true. I'm certainly not advocating biblical compromise for cultural relevancy. But maintaining the status quo is not good stewardship.

I wonder if our lack of creativity stems from a false definition of faithfulness. Let me tell you what faithfulness is not. Faithfulness is *not* doing it the way it's always been done. Faithfulness is *not* holding the fort. Faithfulness is *not* defending the status quo. Faithfulness is the courage to incarnate the gospel in creative ways. Faithfulness is experimenting with new ways of doing discipleship. Faithfulness is playing offense for the kingdom even if some Pharisees find it offensive.

I have a conviction that gets me up early and keeps me up late: there are ways of doing church that no one has thought of yet. If we keep trying to meet new challenges with tired old ideas, I'm afraid we'll fade into irrelevant oblivion. What we need is the freedom to experiment. We need to dream God-sized dreams and take God-sized risks. We need to dare to be different.

One of the defining moments in my ministry happened at a Willow Creek Leadership Conference while I was in seminary. I dreamed of planting a church, but I didn't know where to begin. I had more questions than answers. It was during one of the sessions that I had an epiphany. It wasn't something someone said. I just felt that the conference gave me permission to do church differently. Actually, it did more than that. It dared me to be different. And that has made all the difference. I think our vision of meeting in movie theaters at metro stops throughout the DC area was inspired, in part, by the fact that Willow Creek met in a theater during its early days as a church.

I certainly don't want to be different for difference's sake. But I've come to terms with who I am and who I am not. A decade ago I was trying to be a pastor. Now I'm trying to be myself. That is far more challenging, but it's also far more fulfilling.

Don't try to be who you're not. Be yourself. Don't settle for the status quo. Challenge it. Don't do it the way it's always been done. Dare to be different. Nonconformity invites criticism, but that is the only option if you're following in the footsteps of the quintessential nonconformist, Jesus. God doesn't just give us permission to give expression to our uniqueness; He demands it. And the future of the kingdom may depend upon it.

I recently did an interview with *RETH!NK* magazine. Each of their interviews revolves around this question: "What are you rethinking?" Honestly, I'm rethinking everything all the time, so it was a rather lengthy interview.[5] I never want to become a closed system. I never want to feel like I have it all figured out. I never want to quit trying new things. Why? Because God didn't just create us with the capacity to think. He created us with the capacity to *re*think.

When was the last time you thanked God for your metacognitive ability? It's the ability to think about how you think. And it is an amazing gift, especially for those of us who rarely get it right the first time around. Loving God with all your mind doesn't just mean thinking. Loving God with all your mind means rethinking.

Let me give you an example.

The only number goals we set at National Community Church are missions-giving goals. We dream of the day when we're giving millions of dollars to missions, and we'll get there. But we won't get there the old-fashioned way. Sure, we'll keep going on mission trips. We took ten trips last year, and we'll take ten trips next year. Sure, we'll keep challenging our people to give above and beyond the tithe. But is that the only way to raise money for missions? Not if we dare to be different. Not if we're willing to take risks. Not if we're courageous enough to rethink the way we do what we do.

This year Ebenezers will net a hundred thousand dollars' profit. And every penny of that profit goes to missions. So here's a thought: what if we had a whole chain of coffeehouses giving every penny of profit to missions? I'm no CPA, but ten coffeehouses netting in the neighborhood of a hundred grand each would get us to our million-dollar missions-giving goal.

Criticize by Creating

If the kingdom of God had departments, I'd want to work in Research and Development. In fact, one of our core values at National Community Church is this: everything is an experiment.

Our experimental approach to ministry gives us the freedom to fail. We're not afraid of making mistakes. We're afraid of *not* making mistakes, because that means we're not taking enough risks. Every sermon series is a teaching experiment. Every outreach is an evangelism experiment. Every small group is a discipleship experiment. And here's the beautiful thing about that experimental approach: if the experiment doesn't succeed, you haven't failed. Why? Because it was just an experiment. And if it does succeed, then you find ways of doing it even better.

Fortune 500 companies spend billions of dollars on R&D. They know that new innovations aren't optional. Innovation is the key to survival. I think the same is true of the church. Yet when it comes to R&D, we spend pennies on the dollar. That needs to change.

I recently attended a Wedgwood Circle event hosted by my friend Mark Rodgers. The name derives from an eighteenth-century English potter who leveraged his art to impact culture. Josiah Wedgwood created a cameo of a shackled slave kneeling in prayer with these words inscribed around him: "Am I not a man and a brother?"[6] That image pricked the conscience of England. It also captured the imagination of the nation by becoming the rallying image of the British abolition movement.

In the spirit of Josiah Wedgwood, who used his creativity to impact culture, the Wedgwood Circle is a synergistic group of creative thinkers and angel investors who are committed to the renewal of culture via the creation of cultural artifacts celebrating that which is true, good, and beautiful.[7] Strategic investments are made in upstart artists, musicians, and filmmakers who can shape culture in creative and Christlike ways. Think of it as spiritual research and development.

As salt and light, we cannot afford to take potshots at our culture from the comfortable confines of our Christian subculture. If we are to regain our prophetic voice in our culture, the next generation needs to be unleashed to pursue creative callings with missionary zeal. We need Christ followers who love God with all their mind, shaping culture in classrooms, newsrooms, and boardrooms. We need sanctified imaginations writing songs, making movies, drafting policies, and starting nonprofits.

We need fewer commentators and more innovators. We need fewer critics and more creators. We need fewer imitators and more dreamers.

In the immortal words of Michelangelo, criticize by creating.

Idea Stewardship

Take captive every thought to make it obedient to Christ.[8]

Growing up, I always heard this verse interpreted in negative terms. Take sinful thoughts captive and make them obedient to Christ. And that *is* half the battle. But if we see only the negative implications and not the positive possibilities, it becomes a half truth. This verse is not just about capturing sinful thoughts and getting them out of our minds; it's also about capturing creative thoughts and keeping them in our minds. It means stewarding every word, every thought, every impression, and every revelation inspired by the Spirit of God. I call them *God ideas.* And the way we create culture and change culture is by taking those God ideas captive and then turning them into reality via blood, sweat, and tears. There is a first creation when the God idea is conceived. There is a second creation when the dream becomes reality. And there is a lot of hard work in between.

Let me give you an example.

The first Jewish temple ranks as one of the architectural wonders of the ancient world. Built in the tenth century BC, the project's scope was so massive that Solomon employed thirty thousand loggers and eighty thousand stonecutters. More than three thousand foremen managed the seven-year project.[9]

The temple was the epicenter of Judaism. It was the place of sacrifice. It was the place of worship. It was the place of pilgrimage. But like everything else, the temple was once a figment of the imagination. The cumulative history of the Jewish temple can be traced all the way back to an idea in the mind of King David. But it wasn't David's idea.

> *David gave his son Solomon the plans for the portico of the temple, its buildings, its storerooms, its upper parts, its inner rooms and the place of atonement. He gave him the plans of all that the Spirit had put in his mind for the courts of the temple of the Lord.*[10]

I have no idea how God downloaded the plans to David. I don't know if the plans were JPEGs or a PDF. Maybe they were mental images. Maybe they were detailed drawings. But one thing is sure: The plans for the temple were not manufactured in David's mind. The plans for the temple originated with the Spirit of God. The temple wasn't a good idea. It was a God idea. And David took the idea captive. How? By building the temple.

I have a conviction that has become an integral part of my spiritual operating system: I'd rather have one God idea than a thousand good ideas. Good ideas are good. But one God idea can revolutionize your life. One God idea can change the course of history. Why? Because God ideas aren't manufactured in the human mind. They are conceived by the Spirit of God. Is it easy to discern the difference? Absolutely not. I've confused good ideas for God ideas. I've confused bad ideas for God ideas. But I'm convinced of this: one God idea is worth more than a thousand good ideas.

$53,155 Ideas

You never know when or where or how a God idea will be conceived. It might be a sermon or a conversation or a book or a mission trip or a personal tragedy. But whenever or however a God idea is conceived in your mind, you need to take it captive and make it obedient to Christ. God ideas are like melting snowflakes. They are delicate things of beauty, but they have short shelf lives. If you don't capture them, they disappear forever. And the cost of lost opportunities is incalculable.

Bad ideas cost an arm and a leg. Good ideas are a dime a dozen. God ideas? God ideas are worth at least $53,155!

Every December, our staff does a planning retreat to strategize for the next calendar year. We go into the new year with a sermon strategy, discipleship strategy, marketing strategy, missions strategy, and staffing strategy, just to name a few. The planning retreat is our way of doing our due diligence. But I've also learned that our best ideas are not the by-product of human reasoning. They are the by-product of divine revelation.

At our most recent staff planning retreat, our team was discussing our missions strategy over a meal at the Cheesecake Factory. I was somewhere between spicy cashew chicken and banana cream cheesecake with raspberry purée when an idea came out of nowhere. We were brainstorming how we could give more money to missions, when we thought about the steady stream of Christmas catalogs that had been landing in our mailboxes. I'm not sure why and I'm not sure how, but this idea surfaced: *what if we produced a Christmas catalog for missions?* Two weeks later, thanks to the creative ethic and work ethic of our staff, we produced a Christmas catalog for missions. We handed it out during our weekend services and asked NCCers to consider giving a gift to mission for Christmas. The catalog focused on countries where we had taken missions trips that year. And we made the gift options as tangible as possible by defining specific projects for people to give toward.

When everything was said and done, NCCers purchased dozens of Bibles for sex workers in Thailand, thousands of bricks to build an orphanage in Uganda, more than three hundred goats for a village in Ethiopia, and half a dozen huts for elderly widows in Malawi. From a monetary perspective, I guess you could say that idea was worth $53,155. That is the total amount of gifts given. But it was worth far more than that because you can't put a price tag on a soul. Who knows how many Thai sex workers were given the gospel for the first time or how many Ugandan orphans were given a family because of that one God idea? Or to flip the coin, who knows how many Ethiopian children would still be hungry or how many Malawian widows would still be homeless if we hadn't acted on that God idea?

FIRST-CLASS NOTICERS

Devote yourselves to prayer, being watchful and thankful.[11]

The word *watchful* is a throwback to the Old Testament–era practice of sitting on a city wall and keeping watch. Watchmen were the first ones to see attacking armies or traveling traders. They had the best vantage point. They saw things no one else saw. They saw things before others saw them. That is precisely what happens when we pray. We see things no one else sees. And we see things before others see them. Why? Because prayer gives us a God's-eye view. Prayer heightens our awareness and gives us a sixth sense that enables us to perceive spiritual realities.

In their classic book *Geeks and Geezers,* business gurus Warren Bennis and Robert Thomas make an interesting observation about a common denominator among successful leaders in every field. Bennis and Thomas called them *first-class noticers.*

> *Being a first-class noticer allows you to recognize talent, identify opportunities, and avoid pitfalls. Leaders who succeed again and again are geniuses at grasping context. This is one of those characteristics, like taste, that is difficult to break down into its component parts. But the ability to weigh a welter of factors, some as subtle as how very different groups of people will interpret a gesture, is one of the hallmarks of a true leader.*[12]

Prayer turns us into first-class noticers. It helps us see what God wants us to notice. The more you pray, the more you notice. The less you pray, the less you notice. It's as simple as that.

Let me explain how it works from a neurological perspective.

At the base of our brainstem lies a cluster of nerve cells called the reticular activating system (RAS), which monitors our environment. We are constantly bombarded by countless stimuli vying for our attention, and it is the job of the RAS to determine what gets noticed and what goes unnoticed.

So you download a new ringtone. And you'd swear you've never heard it before, but after downloading it, it seems like everybody else has the same ringtone. It's not that lots of people went out and downloaded it when you did. It's the simple fact that when you downloaded that ringtone, it created a category in your RAS. That ringtone went unnoticed by you before you downloaded it, because it wasn't important to you. Once you downloaded the ringtone, the RAS recognized it as relevant.

When you pray for someone or something, it creates a category in your reticular activating system. And now you notice anything related to those prayers. Have you ever noticed that when you pray, coincidences happen? And when you don't, they don't? It's more than coincidence, it's providence. Prayer creates divine opportunities. But prayer also sanctifies the reticular activating system and enables us to see the God-ordained opportunities that are all around us all the time. And once we see them, we have to seize them.

The Aramaic word for "prayer" means "to set a trap."[13]

We often think of prayer as nothing more than words spoken to God, but maybe it's more than that. Prayer is also when God speaks to us through dreams and desires and promptings and impressions and ideas. Prayer is the mechanism whereby God ideas are conceived and captured. And it's our capacity for prayer that will ultimately determine our creative potential.

One way to set prayer traps is by keeping a prayer journal. In my opinion, journaling is one of the most overlooked and underappreciated spiritual disciplines in our multitasking culture. It doesn't matter whether it's scribbling notes in the margin of your Bible or jotting down thoughts in a Moleskine journal that has inspiring quotes at the top of every page. You need to "write down the revelation."[14] For me, it's blogging and twittering what God is doing in my head and in my heart.[15] But one way or another, you have to take it captive. Why? Because one God idea can change the course of history.

THE ETYMOLOGY OF IDEAS

When it comes to getting God ideas, there are no guaranteed formulas. But let me share a few practical lessons I've learned over the years. These aren't prescriptions. They are descriptions of what's worked for my unique personality and physiology.

First of all, I get my best ideas early in the morning. The earlier, the better. It's just the way I'm wired. Anything I write after noon isn't worth reading because my mind is too cluttered to write clearly. While I've never tried to quantify it, I'm convinced that 90 percent of my creativity happens before nine in the morning.

Second, I start my day by reading. I start with Scripture because I want to get on God's wavelength. But I also read a wide variety of other books. When I read about something I know nothing about, I'm forcing my synapses to fire in new ways. It gets me out of my mental routine. I think of it as mental stretching.

Finally, my office is where I go to get nothing done. Seriously. I love my office. It has a great view of Union Station. But if I want to get something done, I've got to get out of my normal environment and out of my routine. Here's a little formula I came up with several years ago:

Change of pace + Change of place = Change of perspective

If you want to think new thoughts, then read new things, meet new people, and go new places. Learning about something new forces your mind out of its natural tendencies. Meeting new people challenges your subconscious biases. And going new places makes your mind observe what you typically ignore. That's one reason why mission trips, leadership conferences, and church retreats can be so life changing. Geography affects spirituality. I get some of my best ideas at thirty thousand feet, especially if I'm in an exit row.

I subscribe to Arthur McKinsey's school of thought:

If you think of a…problem as being like a medieval walled city, then a lot of people will attack it head on, like a battering ram. They will storm the gates and try to smash through the defenses with sheer intellectual power and brilliance.…

*I just camp outside the city. I wait. And I think. Until one
day—maybe after I've turned to a completely different problem—
the drawbridge comes down and the defenders say, "We surrender."
The answer to the problem comes all at once.*[16]

When I retrace the etymology of ideas in my own life, I'm amazed at
how many of them came to me when I was outside the walls. They didn't
happen in the office or during a meeting. I got outside my normal environment. And the mental drawbridge came down.

Our free market system of small groups at National Community
Church was *not* the by-product of a brainstorming session with our discipleship department. I read a book titled *Dog Training, Fly Fishing, and
Sharing Christ in the 21st Century* while sipping a vanilla chai at Bagels &
Baguettes. I started reading that book and didn't stop until I had finished
it about four hours later. Our discipleship pastor read it the next day. And
the result was a complete overhaul of our small group system. We transi-
tioned from a centralized to a decentralized system. We don't tell our leaders what to do. Sure, we take them through training and hold them
accountable to the covenant they sign. But we expect them to get a vision
from God and go for it. It's less organized and more organic. It's less con-
trolled and more creative. And I believe it's the key to our future growth
as a church. Why? Because God won't grow us beyond our ability to disciple people. And small groups are the primary way we do that at NCC.
So we trust our leaders. We empower our leaders. And most importantly,
we give them the freedom to fail.

Every guest at National Community Church receives a welcome
booklet that looks like a popcorn box. It even has a popcorn-scented
scratch-and-sniff on the front. That piece creatively conveys who we are,
where we've been, and where we're headed as a church. It is the first step

in our assimilation process. And we give away thousands of copies every year. But it all traces back to a Catalyst Conference. I got the idea from a really cool annual report I spotted while wandering the exhibition booths.

We brand our sermon series at NCC. We produce a graphic design that we project on the theater screen. And we produce trailers to promote the series. Just as the medieval church used stained glass to tell the gospel story through pictures, we turn the screen into postmodern stained glass via moving pictures. Where did the idea originate? While I was watching previews and munching on popcorn. Movies are promoted via trailers. Why not sermon series? Especially if a church meets in a movie theater.

The origins of those ideas were very different—a book, an exhibition booth, a movie trailer. But all those ideas have one thing in common: they were conceived outside a normal work environment. Somehow we have to get outside our routines, outside our assumptions, outside our biases. And one way to do that is to get outside the city walls. Or in the case of Habakkuk, climb the city walls.

> I will climb up to my watchtower
>   and stand at my guardpost.
> There I will wait to see what the LORD says.[17]

Everyone needs a watchtower. You need a place to go where you can get out of your routine. It doesn't have to be far away. It might be as close as your closet. But it needs to be someplace where you get good reception. One of my watchtowers is the observation gallery at the National Cathedral. The 360-degree panoramic view of the nation's capital gives me fresh perspective. It also helps me dream God-sized dreams. Another one of my watchtowers is the rooftop of Ebenezers. I hear God's voice more clearly up there.

Where do you go to get perspective? What places help you dream bigger dreams? Where do you go to hear the voice of God more clearly?

Thomas Edison sat in his thinking chair with a metal ball bearing in each palm. Henry David Thoreau skipped stones on Walden Pond. Alexander Graham Bell had a "dreaming place" in a hollow of trees overlooking the Grand River. And George Washington Carver took early morning walks through the woods.

WIRELESS TELEGRAPH STATIONS

George Washington Carver is considered one of the greatest scientific minds of the twentieth century, despite an uphill academic climb. He was accepted by Highland College, then rejected by Highland College when he showed up and they discovered he was an African American. He studied art and piano at Simpson College in Iowa. Then he earned his master's degree in botany from Iowa State University. Upon graduation, Carver accepted a position at Tuskegee University, where he taught for forty-seven years.

Around the turn of the twentieth century, the agricultural economy of the South was suffering. The boll weevil was devastating cotton crops. And the soil was being depleted of nutrients because farmers planted cotton year in and year out. It was George Washington Carver who introduced the concept of crop rotation. He encouraged farmers to plant peanuts, and they did. The strategy revived the soil, but farmers were frustrated because there was no market for peanuts. Their abundant peanut crops rotted in warehouses. When they complained to Carver, he did what he had always done. He prayed about it.

Carver routinely got up at 4:00 a.m., walked through the woods, and asked God to reveal the mysteries of nature. He interpreted Job 12:7–8 literally:

Ask the animals, and they will teach you,
   or the birds of the air, and they will tell you;
or speak to the earth, and it will teach you....

Carver literally asked God to reveal the mysteries of nature. And God did.

Here it is in Carver's own words:

I said, "Lord, why did you make the universe?"

   The Lord replied, "Ask for something more in proportion to that little mind of yours."

   "Then why did you make the earth, Lord?" I asked.

   "Your little mind still wants to know far too much," replied God.

   "Why did you make man, Lord?" I asked.

   "Far too much. Far too much. Ask again," replied God.

   "Explain to me why you made plants, Lord," I asked.

   "Your little mind still wants to know far too much."

   So I meekly asked, "Lord, why did you make the peanut?"

   And the Lord said, "For the modest proportions of your mind, I will grant you the mystery of the peanut. Take it inside your laboratory and separate it into water, fats, oils, gums, resins, sugars, starches and amino acids. Then recombine these under my three laws of compatibility, temperature and pressure. Then you will know why I made the peanut."[18]

On January 20, 1921, George Washington Carver testified before the House Ways and Means Committee on behalf of the United Peanut Association of America. The committee chairman, Joseph Fordney of Michigan, told him he had ten minutes. An hour and forty minutes later, the committee told George Washington Carver he could come back anytime he wanted. Carver mesmerized the committee by demonstrating dozens of uses for the peanut. In the end, Carver discovered more than three hundred uses for the peanut. Or maybe more accurately, the Lord revealed more than three hundred uses. They included everything from glue to shaving cream to soap to insecticide to cosmetics to wood stains to fertilizer to linoleum to the secret sauce in Batterson burgers: Worcestershire sauce.

"To me," said Carver, "nature in its varied forms are the little windows through which God permits me to commune with him, and to see much of his glory, by simply lifting the curtain, and looking in. I love to think of nature as wireless telegraph stations through which God speaks to us every day, every hour, and every moment of our lives."[19]

I love that imagery of nature as a wireless telegraph station. God is always speaking. The real question is whether we are listening. Are we taking those God ideas captive? Are we making them obedient to Christ? What would happen if we took the same approach to life that George Washington Carver took with the peanut?

As Carver said, "Anything will give up its secrets if you love it enough. Not only have I found that when I talk to the little flower or to the little peanut they will give up their secrets, but I have found that when I silently commune with people they give up their secrets also—if you love them enough."[20]

Is it possible that our lack of ideas is really a lack of love?

God ideas aren't the by-product of genius, they are the by-product of love. The more you love God, the more God reveals. If you love Him enough, not for what He can do but for who He is, then God will give up His secrets. Why? Because that is the essence of love. The more you love, the more you reveal. And there are so many secrets waiting to be revealed.

Beyond Reasonableness

I recently read an interview with best-selling author Yann Martel. Martel grew up an atheist but came to believe in God while writing his prize-winning novel *Life of Pi*. He made an interesting observation about the limits of reason. "Reason is very empowering. Our entire Western Democracies are a meticulous result of reason. But reason is just a tool. It doesn't, in and of itself, give you a reason to use it."

Then he revealed something that resonated with my soul. He revealed what prompted his soul-searching. He said, "I was sick to death of reasonableness."[21]

Have you ever been there? If not, just wait. There comes a moment in our lives when good isn't good enough. There comes a moment when reason is too reasonable. It cannot explain suffering or beauty or love. It cannot produce dreams or visions or ideas. Reason will take you only as far as your mind can go, but no farther. And that isn't far enough. Not if you truly love God. Only holy curiosity will get you where God wants you to go. And it's a place way beyond reasonableness.

The human body has approximately a hundred million sensory receptors that enable us to see, hear, taste, touch, and smell. And while that is amazing, it is not nearly as amazing as the hundred *trillion* synaptic connections that crisscross through our brains. I know numbers like that numb us, but that ratio is revealing. Our ability to imagine things with our mind is far greater than our ability to perceive things with our five senses. Mathematically speaking, the imagination is a million times more powerful than the five senses put together. But both of them fall so far short of who God is and what God is capable of.

So many of us live down to the limit of our hundred million sensory receptors. Call it naturalism. It's the unwillingness to believe that which cannot be quantified with the five senses. Or we live down to the limit of our hundred trillion synaptic connections. Call it rationalism. It is the inability to conceive of things that do not fit within the logical constraints of our left brain. As a result, our soul shrinks to the size of our senses, and our mind shrinks to the size of our logic. We become sensory and rational beings. And for a season, we love having a god that we can measure and manage with our mind. But there will come a point when sensory things and rational things won't satisfy your holy curiosity.

Do you have any God ideas that are being held ransom by reasonableness?

Maybe it's time to do something about it. You owe it to yourself. And more importantly, you owe it to God. One God idea has the potential to make more of a difference than a thousand good ideas. Take yours captive and make it obedience to Christ.

PART 4

THE STRENGTH
OF CHRISTIANITY

8

Sweat Equity

It is not the critic who counts; not the man who points
out how the strong man stumbles, or where the doer of
deeds could have done them better. The credit belongs to
the man who is actually in the arena, whose face is marred
by dust and sweat and blood; who strives valiantly;…who
knows the great enthusiasms, the great devotions; who
spends himself in a worthy cause; who at the best knows
in the end the triumph of high achievement, and who at
the worst, if he fails, at least fails while daring greatly.

—TEDDY ROOSEVELT

A few years ago I took a mission trip to Jamaica. I know what you're
thinking, but God cares about the Caribbean too. And someone's
got to go! In all seriousness, it's not all blue ocean and beautiful beaches.
Many islanders live in third-world conditions while vacationers kick back
and soak up the sun. Our team worked from sunup to sundown building a ministry center for drug and alcohol addicts. It was physically gru-
eling. And our primary task was sanding the cement walls to prepare them
for painting. But here's the catch: We didn't have a sander or sandpaper.
We had to use cement blocks to scrape the cement walls. Have you ever
heard fingernails on a chalkboard? Cement on cement is no better! After
a while, it started getting on my nerves. And then we started getting on
one another's nerves. But then there was a moment I'll never forget. It's a

miracle that I heard His still, small voice over the sound of the cement, but I sensed the Spirit saying, *"Mark, this is music in My ears."*

When I finally collapsed into bed after a long day of good old-fashioned hard work, I was absolutely exhausted. My arms and my ears were sore. But I had a sense of spiritual satisfaction unrivaled by any worship service I've ever experienced. I felt like I had given God every ounce of energy I possessed. I felt like I had loved God with all my strength.

I know God loves the sound of our voices when we sing songs of praise. It's music to His ears. But you know what God loves even more? God loves the smell of your sweat. It stinks to high heaven, but it's a sweet aroma. Your sweat is sacred incense. God loves it when we break a sweat serving His purposes. Our energy turns into beautiful melodies, and it's music in God's ear. It's also the way we build sweat equity in His kingdom.

We've explored what it means to love God with all our heart, soul, and mind. But compassion, wonder, and curiosity aren't enough. Strength is the final frontier. And that is where the quest for the lost soul of Christianity takes us. A heart that breaks for the things that break the heart of God is where love begins. But it doesn't end there. Energy completes the equation.

So what does it mean to love God with all your strength? It means expending tremendous amounts of energy for kingdom causes. It means blood, sweat, and tears. It means servanthood and sacrifice. It means good old-fashioned hard work.

Energy may be the least appreciated dimension of love because it's the least sentimental. But it's the most practical. And how we invest our energy reveals our true priorities. It also reveals how much we love someone. Let me put it in relational terms. For the guys who aren't married yet, here are my premarital counseling CliffsNotes: taking out the garbage is romantic. Why? Because love isn't measured by words spoken. Love is measured by calories burned.

Christianity was never intended to be a noun. And when we turn it into a noun, it becomes a turnoff. Christianity was always intended to be a verb. We've got to act on God ideas. We've got to obey the promptings of the Holy Spirit. We've got to seize opportunities to serve. Talk is cheap, and we have cheapened the gospel long enough. At the end of the day, God isn't going to say, "Well *said*, good and faithful servant." There is only one commendation when everything is said and done: "Well *done*, good and faithful servant."[1] God doesn't reward what we know. He doesn't reward what we say. He rewards the expenditure of energy.

Nothing is more fulfilling than burning calories for a kingdom cause. Anything less than leveraging all our strength for God's purposes is boring at best and hypocritical at worst. So many Christians are so bored. So many Christians are so frustrated by the gap between their theology and reality. The way to close the gap, and the way to experience that holy rush of adrenaline again, is to break a sweat serving others. It can be as simple as baby-sitting for a single mom who needs a night out, serving in a ministry in your local church, or volunteering at a local nursing home. It doesn't matter how big or how small, every calorie burned for a kingdom cause earns compound interest for eternity. And it'll fill the emptiness in your soul with pure joy.

GO. SET. READY.

There is an old adage: "Ready. Set. Go." And I know it's predicated on the importance of preparation. But I think it's backward. You'll never be ready. And you'll never be set. Sometimes you just need to go for it. We need a paradigm shift: Go. Set. Ready.

Some people spend their entire lives getting ready for what God wants them to do. But they never end up doing it because they never come to the realization that they'll never be ready. Listen, you'll never have enough education or enough experience. And you'll never have enough time or enough money. And that is where so many of us get stuck, spiritually. Our failure to act on God ideas not only breeds doubt and discouragement; it's also a form of disobedience. Not acting on a God idea is no less disobedient than breaking one of the Ten Commandments. And when we fail to act on those God ideas, we're playing at half strength. And half strength doesn't cut it when it comes to the Great Commandment.

Don't miss the link between creativity and energy. Most of us are not creative *not* because we're not creative. We're not creative because it's too hard. And we give up too easily. One way to spell creativity is E-N-E-R-G-Y. As Thomas Edison observed, it's 10 percent inspiration and 90 percent perspiration.

"Everyone who's ever taken a shower has had an idea," said Nolan Bushnell. "It's the person who gets out of the shower, dries off, and does something about it who makes a difference." Bushnell knows whereof he speaks. You may not recognize the name, but his imagination may be responsible for some of your memories. He is the creator of the video game system Atari. And he started a chain of more than five hundred Chuck E. Cheese's restaurants, where my kids have celebrated many a birthday party.

The greatest moments in life are those moments when a God idea is conceived in your mind or an epiphany awakens your soul or a sympathy breakthrough breaks your heart. Something comes alive within you. And it's absolutely energizing. But if you don't act on it, the thing that brings you to life will cause a slow, painful death.

For nearly a decade, that's how I felt about writing. I knew I was called to write. In fact, I feel as called to write as I do to pastor. It's not something I want to do. It's something I can't *not* do. But passion turned to frustration because of the curse of perfectionism. I could never seem to finish what I started. So for several years I stopped trying altogether.

My call to write traces back to a defining moment when I was nineteen years old. A preacher named Sam Farina shared a message out of an obscure Old Testament passage about an ancient warrior named Benaiah who chased a lion into a pit on a snowy day and killed it. I don't know how. I don't know why. But that message did more than capture my imagination. Call it an epiphany. Call it a God idea. Call it a calling. This thought was conceived in my spirit: *If I ever write a book, I'd love to write a book about that story.* It took fifteen years and two manuscripts. But I took that thought captive. I held on to it. I nurtured it. I fought for it. And I worked at it. And the dream finally became reality on October 16, 2006, when *In a Pit with a Lion on a Snowy Day* hit bookstores.

That book isn't just a book. It was an act of obedience. I had to take the thought captive. Then I had to make it obedient to Christ by setting my alarm clock early in the morning. God ideas don't become reality without some blood, sweat, and tears. Oh yeah, and loss of sleep. But that's the true test of love, isn't it? If you love someone or something enough, the expenditure of energy isn't seen as a chore. It's a privilege. It's not something you have to do, it's something you get to do. Love turns work into worship. And that's how I view writing. It's worshiping God with a computer keyboard. I wish I could say that each book is easier to write than the one before, but that certainly hasn't been my experience. But the harder it is, the greater the sacrifice of praise.

We have a core value at NCC: Pray like it depends on God and work like it depends on you. Prayer is the first half of the equation. But you can't just pray about it. At some point you need to stop praying and start sweating. And then you need to keep sweating until the God idea becomes reality.

I'm absolutely convinced that the greatest predictor of success in any endeavor is persistence. It's not only how hard you try, it's also how long you try. We tend to overestimate how much we can accomplish in the short term. But we underestimate how much we can accomplish over the long haul. Why? Because energy is exponential. The harder you work and the longer you work, the more it pays off. Energy turns into synergy. And that persistence pays off.

In a study involving Japanese and American first graders, kids were given a difficult puzzle to solve while researchers measured how long they would try before giving up. On average, the American children lasted 9.47 minutes. The Japanese children lasted 13.93 minutes. That is a 47 percent difference.[2]

Want to guess who scores higher on standardized math tests?

Success in any endeavor is a by-product of trying harder and trying longer. There are no substitutes. There are no shortcuts. It doesn't matter whether it's athletics or academics, music or math. Study after study has shown that it takes about ten years or ten thousand hours to become great at anything.[3] No one is a natural. Or maybe I should say, everyone is a natural. But you need to work hard and work long. In the words of Malcolm Gladwell, "Ten thousand hours is the magic number of greatness."[4]

Are there any God ideas you've given up on? Any God-ordained passions that you have stopped fighting for? Any God-sized dreams gathering the dust of disobedience?

Don't give up on them. You need to try. Then you need to try harder. And then you need to try longer.

Go. Set. Ready.

WHY NOT?

I love *Deep Thoughts* by Jack Handey. His tongue-in-cheek humor makes me laugh, but it also makes me think. Here is one of my favorites: "As the light changed from red to green to yellow and back to red again, I sat there thinking about life. Was it nothing more than a bunch of honking and yelling? Sometimes it seemed that way."

One of my pet peeves is people sitting at green lights. If you don't put the pedal to the metal when the light turns green, I'm going to give you a little love tap. Why? Because I've got places to go and things to do. Life is too short to sit at green lights.

Two thousand years ago, Jesus said, "Go."[5] So why do we operate with a red-light mentality? It seems like many of us are waiting for the green light we've already been given. Let me put it in practical terms with a personal example. NCC is a multisite church. Our vision is to meet in movie theaters at metro stops throughout the DC area. And launching new locations is part of our DNA. But at first there was a little resistance to the idea. Some people asked, "Why?" And on one level, that is a fair question. But I honestly think it's the wrong question. The real question is, "Why not?" Why wouldn't we continue to launch new locations and try to reach more people? Why wouldn't we continue to invest in what God is blessing?

As Christ followers, we need to take a *why not* approach to life. It dares to dream. It's bent toward action. And it's not looking for excuses *not* to do something.

Don't get me wrong. I've agonized with plenty of people when it comes to discerning the will of God. I know it's a painful process. Even after prayer and fasting, it usually involves a difficult decision. And I'm certainly not advocating a thoughtless or prayerless approach to decision making. You need to know that God is calling you to devote your life to missions or take the internship offer or quit your job or make the move. But I wonder if we're so afraid of doing the wrong thing that we never do the right thing.

Here is one of the great ironies and great dangers of loving God with your mind. You have to think and rethink, but you cannot overthink. And there is a fine line between rethinking and overthinking. But here is what I know for sure: overanalysis always results in spiritual paralysis. If you try to logically figure out the will of God, you'll never take a step of faith. Why? Because the will of God is not logical. It's theological. It adds God into the equation, and that's why it doesn't always add up on our human calculators. The promptings of the Holy Spirit won't always make sense to your logical left brain. In fact, God ideas often seem like bad ideas. But that is when you need to allow the Holy Spirit to override your intellect.

SPIRIT PROMPTINGS

A few years ago I had a meeting with Dr. George Wood, the general super-intendent of the Assemblies of God. I had never been in his office before, so my natural instinct was to check out the books on his shelves and the paintings on his walls. One painting in particular caught my attention. It was a large framed painting of an African man standing on a high hillside overlooking the ocean. There was a large steamship on the horizon and a smaller canoe coming toward the shoreline. I was intrigued by the paint-ing, so I asked George to share the backstory.

In 1908, John Perkins and his wife were on board a steamship round-ing the coast of Liberia. They knew God had called them to Africa, but they didn't know exactly where God wanted them to go. As the ship made its way around Garraway Bay, they sensed the Holy Spirit prompting them to get off the ship.

Unknown to the Perkinses, there was a young man living in that region named Jasper Toe. He was a God-fearing man who practiced his tribal rituals, but he'd never heard the name of Jesus. One night he looked into the night sky and said, "If there is a God in heaven, help me find

You." As Jasper stood under the stars, a voice he'd never heard before said, *"Go to Garraway Beach. You will see a box on the water, with smoke coming out of it. And from that box on the water will come some people in a small box. These people in this small box will tell you how to find Me."*

Jasper Toe traveled seven days on foot to Garraway Beach, arriving on Christmas Day, 1908. From the shore he saw a black box floating on the water with smoke coming out of it, also known as a steamship. And that is when John Perkins and his wife sensed the Holy Spirit saying, *"Get off the ship here. This is where I want you to go."*

When they went to the captain of the ship and asked him to let them get off the ship, he said, "I can't let you off the boat here. This is cannibal country. People go in there and never come back."

John Perkins insisted, "God wants us to get off the boat."

The captain stopped the steamship. He put them in a mammy chair that swung them over the side of the ship. Then the Perkinses and all of their belongings were put into a canoe, and they rowed to shore in that little box. When they got to the shore, Jasper Toe was waiting to welcome them. He motioned for them to follow him and they did. They could not speak each other's language, but the Perkinses followed Jasper Toe through the interior all the way back to his village. They eventually learned the language. They started the first church in that village. And Jasper Toe was their first convert.

Those who knew him at the end of his life described Jasper Toe as one of the godliest men they'd ever met. And his legacy is the hundreds of churches he led as the first superintendent of the Assemblies of God in Liberia.

What if the Perkinses had ignored the prompting of the Holy Spirit? What if they had dismissed that God idea as a bad idea? What if they had asked "Why?" instead of "Why not?" What if they had decided to play it safe and stay on the ship?

I'm sure God could have intervened in another way. And I certainly believe the sovereignty of God is bigger than our indecision. If you think that your indecisions or bad decisions can somehow foil the eternal plans of almighty God, then your view of God is way too small. But God has given us a free will. And it begs the question: what if the Perkinses had decided not to go when God gave them the green light?

Well, if that steamship had not stopped and the Perkinses had not gotten off, it seems to me that Jasper Toe would have taken a long walk for nothing. And if God had given him another vision, I wonder if he would have bothered to respond to it. I would like to think that God would have intervened in another way. But who can calculate the opportunity costs when we ignore the promptings of the Spirit, thereby missing divine appointments?

Faith is not faith until it is acted upon. That is the litmus test. Faith without works is dead.[6] So is love without energy.

THE GREAT OMISSION

I wonder if the negative perception that many people have of the church stems from the negative energy we project. And I wonder if our negative energy stems from our negative view of righteousness. We falsely view righteousness as doing nothing wrong. So we practice holiness by subtraction. "Don't do this. Don't do that. And you're okay." But the problem with that approach is this: you can do nothing wrong and still do nothing right. Goodness is not the absence of badness. And righteousness means more than doing nothing wrong. It means doing something right.

Do you really think God's ultimate dream for us is doing nothing wrong? Is God's ultimate plan a weekly pilgrimage to the pew? Is God's highest aim the absence of sin?

As a parent, I love it when my kids make a difficult decision to not do something wrong. But the thing that brings me far more joy is seeing them pursue God-given passions and go after God-sized dreams. I want them to maximize their God-given potential for His purposes. And that is God's ultimate desire for each of us. Potential is God's gift to us. What we do with it is our gift to God.[7]

I wonder if we have forgotten that there are two kinds of sin. A sin of commission is doing something you should not have done. In other words, it's breaking a prohibitive commandment. And I'm certainly against sins of commission. But we've fixated on sins of commission long enough. You want to know what I think really grieves the heart of our heavenly Father? It's the sins of omission. It's all the things we would have, could have, and should have done for the cause of Christ but did not do.

In God's economy, breaking even is a total loss. Isn't that the lesson in the parable of the talents? The servant with one talent broke even, and in my estimation that's not half bad. But Jesus called him a "wicked, lazy servant."[8] Can I make a confession? That seems a little harsh to me. Part of me feels like Jesus should tone it down. But I've learned that when I think Jesus is wrong, it actually reveals what's wrong with me. In this instance it reveals my incomplete and inadequate view of righteousness. The greatest risk is taking no risks. And it's not just risky, it's wrong. Righteousness is using all of our God-given gifts to their full God-given potential.

Love doesn't play it safe; it takes risks. Love doesn't make excuses; it takes responsibility. Love doesn't see problems; it seizes opportunities to step up and step in. The Greek word for "strength" means "the antithesis of apathy." And Jesus is the ultimate example.

HOLY TEMPLE TANTRUM

If I were to ask you to close your eyes and picture Jesus, what image would come to your mind? For me, it's a rather demure Jesus with a lamb draped around His neck. That is my oldest mental image of Jesus, probably because that is the painting that hung in my grandparents' house. Is it an accurate picture? Absolutely. But it's an incomplete picture. Yes, Jesus was meek and mild. But He also had a wild side.

One of my favorite episodes in the gospels is when Jesus throws a holy temple tantrum. I wish an artist could capture the fire in His eyes or the flex in His muscles. He turned over tables. He threw out the money-changers. And He did it while wielding a whip He Himself had made. Jump back, Indiana Jones!

I love the way Dorothy Sayers described the wild side of His personality.

> To do them justice, the people who crucified Jesus did not do so because he was a bore. Quite the contrary; he was too dynamic to be safe. It has been left for later generations to muffle up that shattering personality and surround Him with an atmosphere of tedium. We have declawed the lion of Judah and made Him a housecat for pale priests and pious old ladies.[9]

I would love to have seen the look on the disciples' faces when Jesus threw down. I think their jaws dropped. But it also jogged their memories.

> Then his disciples remembered this prophecy from the Scriptures: "Passion for God's house will consume me."[10]

Jesus wasn't just the wisest or kindest person who ever lived. He was also the most passionate. In fact, the final week of His life sets the standard. It is known as *the Passion*. And it's epitomized by the drops of blood that came out of His holy pores as He agonized over going to the cross.

Our love for God is expressed in sweat. His love for us was expressed in bloody sweat.

Those who follow in the footsteps of Christ ought to be the most passionate people on the planet. The word *enthusiasm* comes from a combination of two Greek words: *en* and *Theos*. It means "in God." And the more you get into God, the more passionate you become. As we learn to love God with all our strength, He doesn't crucify our desires. He sanctifies them and intensifies them. God doesn't find our desires too strong. He finds them too weak. In the words of C. S. Lewis, "We are half-hearted creatures fooling around with drink and sex and ambition when infinite joy is offered us."

Sin is a waste of energy. Plain and simple. It's wasting your energy on things you can't have or can't control. And it's actually a double waste. After you waste your energy on things like lust and pride and anger, then you have to waste even more energy on things like guilt and shame and regret. Nothing is more de-energizing than sin. But by the same token, nothing is more reenergizing than obedience. It's pure energy.

No one was more energetic than Jesus. He cast out demons, healed the sick, loved the outcasts, and taught the crowds. And He did all of that while defending Himself against the Pharisees and dealing with the insecurities and ineptitudes of His own disciples. Of course, that's not to mention the miles He logged hiking mountainous terrain. Or the fact that He got up early, stayed up late, and pulled all-nighters. So the obvious question is this: where did all that energy come from? The answer is found in a fascinating dialogue.

> *His disciples urged him, "Rabbi, eat something."*
> *But he said to them, "I have food to eat that you know nothing about."*

> *Then his disciples said to each other, "Could someone have*
> *brought him food?"*
>
> *"My food," said Jesus, "is to do the will of him who sent me and*
> *to finish his work."*[11]

The point Jesus made went right over the heads of the disciples, and I think it goes right over our heads too. When you read "food," you need to think *energy* because that's what it is. Food is a source of energy. It has caloric value. And Jesus makes a profound point here: the will of God is energizing. That's what I felt after scraping those concrete walls in Jamaica. That's what I feel after preaching at our weekend services. That's what I feel after one of our servant evangelism outreaches.

So how do you stay energized? Stay in the will of God. And not just in the negative sense of not committing sins of commission. If sin is the way we waste energy, then pursuing God-ordained passions and going after God-sized dreams is the way we produce energy. Nothing is more energizing.

THE LAW OF ENTROPY

The second law of thermodynamics states this physical truth: if left to its own devices, everything in the universe moves toward disorder and decay.

Cars rust. Food rots. And, of course, the human body ages.

It's also called the *law of entropy.* And the only way to prevent entropy is to introduce an outside energy source to counteract it. The technical term for this is *negentropy.* And the refrigerator is a good example. You plug it into an electrical outlet, and it produces cold air that keeps food from rotting. If the refrigerator gets disconnected from its energy source, entropy will take over again. And things will get smelly. Unfortunately, I know this from personal experience. We returned from Christmas vacation a few years ago and discovered a dead refrigerator that smelled like a dead animal. If your refrigerator dies, I highly recommend keeping the door closed.

Isn't that what happens when we get disconnected from God? Life moves toward decay and disorder. So how do we overcome our entropic tendencies? I think the answer is found in one of my favorite verses. If sin is entropy, then investing our energies in a God-sized vision is negentropy.

Where there is no vision, the people perish.[12]

The word *perish* comes from the Hebrew word *para,* and "entropy" is a fair translation. It refers to the process of decay. More specifically, it can be used to describe perishable food that is past its prime. In other words, rotting food.

When I was a freshman at the University of Chicago, my grandmother sent me a home-baked apple pie. My popularity rating instantly skyrocketed. For a brief window of time, everyone in my dorm wanted to be my friend. But I didn't want any friends. I wanted my grandmother's pie. So I hid the last piece of pie under my bed. Then I totally forgot about it.

Two months later, my roommate and I started smelling a strange odor. If you've lived in a dorm, you know that isn't altogether abnormal. But when the odor started seeping under our door and into the hallway, we decided to do something about it. We turned our dorm room upside down. When I finally looked under my bed, I discovered the law of entropy. If left to its own devices, apple pie will turn into a greenish glob of moldy goo. Of course, I then went door to door offering that last piece of pie to everyone in my dorm.

That rotten piece of apple pie is a picture of Proverbs 29:18. Where there is no vision, we become a greenish glob of moldy goo. Why? Because where there is no vision, entropy takes over. Vision acts as a preservative. It keeps us young. It keeps us energized. It keeps us on the offensive.

I have a theory: most church problems don't come from the abundance of sin but rather from the lack of vision. I'm not suggesting that there aren't sin problems or that those sin problems aren't serious. But in too many instances, there isn't enough vision to keep churches busy. Our vision isn't big enough to demand all our energies, so we manufacture petty problems to keep us busy. I think the same is true on a personal level. If we had a larger vision of what God wanted to accomplish in us and through us, our petty problems would cease to exist because they would cease to be important.

Too often we try to stop sinning by not sinning. But that is a losing battle. It's what psychologists call a *double bind.* Let me give you an example: *be spontaneous.* You can't do it, can you? Why? Because I told you to. In a similar sense, *don't sin* is a double bind. Of course, you can try to stop sinning by not sinning. And when that doesn't work, you can try even harder to stop sinning by not sinning. But what you need is a vision from God that captures your imagination and consumes your energy.

Vision is the cure for sin. A God-given vision keeps us from decay and disorder. It energizes everything we do. And turning that vision into reality is one way we love God with all our strength.

STREET SENSE

Breaking a sweat for a God-given vision is the key to fulfillment and fruitfulness. It's also the difference between making a living and making a life.

Laura Osuri had a great job working for a great newspaper, but something was missing. Her job was just a job. Then she got a vision. What if she leveraged her journalism skills to help the homeless? That God idea became reality in the form of the weekly newspaper *Street Sense,* with the tag line "Where the poor and homeless earn and give their two cents." Distributing that newspaper on urban street corners doesn't just give the homeless an income; it also gives them an outlet. After our media department profiled her story during one of our services at NCC, a homeless member of our congregation caught me afterward. He showed me an article he had written for the latest edition of *Street Sense* and said, "I'm an author too." He couldn't have been more proud. I couldn't have been more proud either.

I can't help but wonder how many of us have a God-sized dream within us but we're so afraid of failing that we never even try. We can't imagine how the God idea could possibly happen. It's beyond reasonableness. So we never act on the vision. Here's a challenge: don't worry about the outcome. That isn't your responsibility. He who began a good work is the One who will carry it to completion.[13] You simply need to act on it. It doesn't have to be something big. In fact, it will probably be something small. But if you do little things like they are big things, God will bless them and use them.

When my son Parker turned twelve, I took him through a yearlong discipleship journey. It started with a discipleship covenant that included a spiritual, intellectual, and physical challenge. And it culminated with a choreographed birthday celebration involving three of his uncles. I took Parker kayaking on the Potomac River on his birthday. What he didn't know was that his uncles were hiding out on Roosevelt Island awaiting our arrival. When Parker docked his kayak, each uncle took him for a walk and gave him a gift. The gifts he received corresponded to the four values we came up with as part of the spiritual challenge: humility, generosity, gratitude, and courage. I'll save the details for another book at another time, but let me mention one of the gifts. It was actually a regift. Parker received a fifty-dollar bill with one stipulation: he couldn't use it for himself. I challenged him to multiply it and use it for something he cared about.

A few weeks later I asked Parker what he might want to do with the money. To be perfectly honest, I wasn't sure he'd have any ideas. So I was pleasantly surprised when he immediately said he wanted to help kids in Africa. I told him we might want to narrow that down a little bit, and he named the country of Kenya. I think the genesis of his idea was a school-sponsored program raising money to buy cows for poor villages in Africa. And that idea led to this idea: kids for kids. Parker said he wanted to use his money, and the money others had given to him, to buy baby goats for kids in Kenya. I immediately contacted a couple from National Community Church who were serving as missionaries in Kenya. They told us that chickens might be more efficient and effective than goats. So to make a long story short, there is now a village in Kenya with a chicken farm, thanks to my son.

I know I sound like a proud parent. And I am. But I don't think it begins to compare with the pride our heavenly Father feels when we act compassionately and creatively on behalf of others. I cried when I got the pictures of African children proudly holding their chickens in their arms. Imagine the tears of joy our heavenly Father sheds when we love Him by serving others, when we act on the ideas He inspired, when we break a sweat for a kingdom cause.

It blesses Him more than the people we bless. And it blesses us too.

So don't just point out problems; be the solution. Don't just criticize what's wrong; do something right. Quit living as if the purpose of life is to arrive safely at death. Go after a dream that is destined to fail without divine intervention.

Break a sweat.

9

The Hammer of
a Higher God

A low view of God is the cause of a hundred lesser evils. A high view of God is the solution to ten thousand temporal problems.

—A. W. TOZER

Most of us remember speeches or sermons or lectures because of *what* was said. Not this one. This particular lecture was memorable because of *where* it was delivered. I was taking a physics class as a freshman at the University of Chicago. I had spent most of the semester nodding, not in agreement with what my professor was saying but in a colossal struggle to stay awake during the postlunch time slot. Then my professor revealed something that transformed an ordinary lecture hall into hallowed scientific ground. He informed our class that our lecture hall was located just a few feet from the infamous squash court where Enrico Fermi unleashed the power of the atom by splitting it on December 2, 1942. The technical term is *nuclear fission*. And the full impact of that discovery was felt on August 6, 1945, when the *Enola Gay* dropped the world's first atomic bomb over Hiroshima, Japan.

It took forty-three seconds for the bomb to fall thirty-one thousand feet from the B-29 bomber. At nineteen hundred feet above the ground, a barometric switch triggered the first subatomic chain reaction. In just a few millionths of a second, that chain reaction went through eighty generations of doubling. The bomb reached a temperature of several million degrees Celsius, the temperature at the core of the sun. When the bomb exploded at 8:16:02 local time, four square miles of the city were instantly and completely devastated. Buildings were leveled and hilltops scorched six miles away. Glass was broken up to twelve miles away. And the bomb produced so much energy that the glare from the blast would have been visible from Jupiter, roughly 390 million miles away.

As if that isn't staggering enough, here is what is almost inconceivable. The energy produced by that bomb was the by-product of a subatomic reaction that used only 1 percent of two pounds of uranium. One-third of one ounce of uranium was translated into an explosion two thousand times more powerful than that of any bomb in the history of warfare up to that time.

It seems like a gross understatement, but there is an awful lot of energy in a very small amount of matter. And if the amount of energy in one-third of one ounce of uranium is virtually inconceivable, then how can we even begin to comprehend the potential energy of the omnipotent Creator who created all matter?

The truth is, we can't. That is the point of Paul's prayer in Ephesians 1:18–21:

> *I pray…that the eyes of your heart may be enlightened in order that you may know the hope to which he has called you, the riches of his glorious inheritance in the saints, and his incomparably great power for us who believe. That power is like the working of his mighty strength, which he exerted in Christ when he raised him from the dead and seated him at his right hand in the heavenly realms, far above all rule and authority, power and dominion, and every title that can be given, not only in the present age but also in the one to come.*

Paul combines two Greek superlatives, *huper* and *megas,* to describe God's power. His power isn't just incomparable. His power isn't just great. It is *incomparably great.* In other words, there is no comparison point.

None of us can imagine what God is capable of. Which means none of us can imagine what we're capable of if we give God control of our lives. His power sets off a chain reaction. And with His energy at work within us, there is nothing we cannot do. Unfortunately, our lives don't always reflect that reality.

God loves it when we break a sweat for a kingdom cause, but exerting our own strength isn't enough. Loving God with all our strength is living in His strength. But many of us never flip the switch. We never receive the power He promised.[1] And without His power, we become nothing more than theological Christians. Our testimony is reduced to our words. Our impact is reduced to our abilities. And not only is that less than exciting, it's wrong. Without His power at work within us, we cannot accomplish His purposes.

The quest for the lost soul of Christianity is about rediscovering the primal energy that sustained the first-century church during persecution. It's about rediscovering the primal energy that propelled them to take the gospel to the four corners of the ancient world. It's about rediscovering the primal energy that empowered them to do miracles in Jesus' name.

$E = MC^2$

I am absolutely convinced that our biggest problem is our small view of God. Every other problem is a symptom. A small view of God is the cause of all lesser problems. A big view of God is the cure.

On a bad day, we tend to reduce God to the size of our greatest failure, biggest problem, or worst fear. On a good day, we tend to reduce God to the size of our greatest gift, highest hope, or best attribute. But either way, we are creating God in our image. And what we end up with is a supersized version of ourselves. A god who is just a little bigger, a little stronger, and a little wiser than we are. But in reality God is *infinitely* better than your best thought on your best day. In fact, your best thought on your best day is at least 15.3 billion light-years short of how good and how great God really is.[2]

So what does a small view of God have to do with loving God with all your strength? Well, at its core, loving God with all your strength really means loving God with all *His* strength. It's not about what you can do for God. It's about what God can do in you and through you. Few things are more thrilling than doing what you didn't think could be done. And it's not just thrilling for you. It's thrilling for God. Like a proud parent, our heavenly Father loves it when we do impossible things by His power and for His glory. Loving God with all your strength is living in raw dependence upon His power. And when you live in raw dependence upon His power, you will do things that cannot be done.

The word for "strength" that Paul used in his prayer is the same word that Jesus used in the Great Commandment. It refers to supernatural strength beyond natural ability. The moment you put your faith in Christ, the best you can do is no longer the best *you* can do. The best you can do is the best *God* can do.

You enter into the kingdom of infinite possibilities. And living beyond the limits of human capacity isn't just incredibly exciting; it's the way you love God with all your strength. Or, I should say, His strength.

A century ago, Albert Einstein published what may be the most recognizable equation in science: $E = MC^2$. Energy equals mass multiplied by the speed of light, squared. Think of mass as sweat equity. It's the energy we invest in kingdom causes. And without our expenditure of energy, nothing happens. But the real key to the equation is light. And God is light.[3] Think of light squared as His power at work within us. It's

His power that completes the equation. He empowers us, enables us, and energizes us. And our human effort plus His divine power equals supernatural synergy.

DOING VERSUS RECEIVING

Here is the great irony when it comes to loving God. And maybe I should have revealed this at the very beginning of the book, because this is the crux of the matter. In and of ourselves, we're not capable of loving God. We cannot manufacture love for Him. We can only respond to His love for us. And I hope that sets you free. Religion is all about doing things for God. Christianity is all about receiving what Christ has done for us on the cross. And what we do for God is a reflection of and response to what God has done for us.

A few years ago I went through an intense season of discouragement. I'm an extremely upbeat person, so I don't get too down for too long. But during that time, I hit bottom and I didn't bounce. So I did what I always do when I'm in a spiritual slump. I followed the timeless advice of Revelation 2:5:

Do the things you did at first.

I decided to go back to a primal spiritual practice. I did a forty-day fast. And I decided to fast from television because I felt like I needed to tune out the white noise in my life so I could tune in the voice of the Spirit. During those forty days, I devoted more time than usual to prayer. But I sensed the Spirit saying to my spirit, *"Mark, Me hearing your voice isn't nearly as important as you hearing My voice."* So I bought a new Bible and read it cover to cover in forty days. That Bible, with all of its underlined verses and margin notes, is one of my prized possessions today.

During those forty days, God spoke to me more frequently and more clearly than at any time previously. I think I had an acute appreciation for His voice because I was coming out of a season when God seemed silent. And one of the things the Lord spoke to me during that time has become a personal mantra: *It's not about what you can do for God; it's about what God has done for you.* That truth changed my life. Yes, I still have days when I'm striving in my own strength. But I am quickly reminded of the verse that inspired that thought. It's now one of my favorite verses. And it's one of the most freeing verses in the Bible.

> *Embracing what God does for you is the best thing you can do for him.*[4]

The most primal form of love is *not* doing things for God. It is receiving with gratitude what He has already done for us. And then reflecting it in our lives.

Let me put it in scientific terms.

Albedo is the measurement of how much light a celestial body reflects. Our night-light, the moon, has an albedo of 0.07. In other words, 7 percent of the light that strikes the moon's surface is reflected. Enceladus, a moon of Saturn, has the highest albedo of any celestial body in our solar system. It reflects 99 percent of the light that hits its surface. In a similar sense, we are called to reflect God—His compassion, His wonder, His creativity, and His energy. You cannot manufacture those things. You can only reflect them. Our love for God is nothing more and nothing less than a reflection of God's love for us.

ULTRASOUND

To fully appreciate God's incomparably great power, we have to go all the way back to God's first words: "Let there be light."[5] God speaks, and the first sound waves don't just travel through space, they create it. Light waves begin to defeat darkness at a rate of 186,000 miles per second.

When we hear the word *said*, we tend to think in linguistic terms. But if you want to fully appreciate the first words of God, you need to think in terms of physics. Sound isn't just language. It is first and foremost a form of energy. The word *said* might be better translated "challenge" in the context of creation. God challenges the darkness. And darkness is defeated by light.

Scientifically speaking, the human voice is simply sound waves with different frequencies that travel through air at 1,125 feet per second. The average male speaks at a frequency of about 100 hertz, and the average female has a higher-pitched voice at about 200 hertz. You've got your Barry Whites and Mariah Careys, who have lower- and higher-pitched voices, but the vocal range for humans is between 55 and 880 hertz. And that means that our voices are pretty much good for one thing: communication. We use our voices to sing or shout or speak. But not God. His vocal range knows no limits.

Just as our vocal capacity is limited to a relatively small range between 55 and 880 hertz, so our range of hearing is limited to sound waves between 20 and 20,000 hertz. Anything below 20 hertz is infrasonic for humans. Anything above 20,000 hertz is ultrasonic. Anything outside that range is inaudible to us, but that is when the power of sound is truly revealed.

Infrasound has the capacity to cause headaches and earthquakes. According to zoologists, infrasound helps elephants predict changes in weather and helps birds navigate as they migrate. Infrasound can also be used to locate underground oil or predict volcanic eruptions.

On the other end of the sound spectrum, ultrasound has the power to kill insects, track submarines, break glass, perform noninvasive surgery, topple buildings, clean jewelry, catalyze chemical reactions, heal damaged tissues, pasteurize milk, break up kidney stones, drill through hard materials, and of course give you the first glimpse of your unborn son or daughter via sonogram.

There is a lot more to sound than meets the ear. And God's ability to speak isn't limited to our ability to hear. God doesn't just use words to communicate, He uses His voice to heal and reveal and convict and create. Like infrasonic and ultrasonic sound waves, His words are full of power. And they never return void.[6]

I know most people would claim that they have never heard the voice of God. And that may be true on one level. You may have never heard His audible voice between 55 and 880 hertz. But you have *seen* His voice. The universe was structured by His acoustic oscillations. Everything you see was once a sound wave in the vocal cords of God. When you look at creation, you are hearing with your eyes an echo of the Creator's voice.

> *By the word of the LORD were the heavens made....*
> *For he spoke, and it came to be.*[7]

Less than a century ago, the prevailing opinion in cosmology was that the Milky Way galaxy was the sum total of the universe. Nineteenth-century Austrian physicist Christian Doppler had theorized an expanding universe, but there wasn't much tangible evidence to back up his belief. Then an astronomer named Edwin Hubble spied several spiral nebulae that were far too distant to be part of the Milky Way galaxy. The announcement of his discovery on January 1, 1925, was an astronomical paradigm shift. He discovered that the degree of redshift observed in light coming from other galaxies increased in proportion to the distance of that galaxy from the Milky Way. In other words, the universe is still expanding. Which means that the original "Let there be light" is still creating galaxies at the outer edges of the universe. Amazing thought, isn't it? Billions of galaxies trace their origin to four words.

Now let me ask you a question. If God can create billions of galaxies with four words, what *can't* He do?

The same voice that spoke order into chaos at the dawn of creation is still doing it. He can speak order into the chaos of your life. He can speak light into your darkness. He can bring back to life the parts of you that have died. And it doesn't even take four words. Sometimes all it takes is one touch.

The Laying On of Hands

My friend and mentor Dick Foth defines *love* as "the accurate assessment and adequate supply of another person's need." Sometimes love is expressed via heart, soul, or mind. A kind act, an encouraging word, or a heartfelt prayer is enough. But there are moments when love manifests itself as raw primal power. The woman with the issue of blood didn't need Jesus to say nice things to her or about her. She didn't need a get-well card or flowers. What she needed most was a healing touch. And one touch is all it took to end twelve years of chronic pain.

> *A large crowd followed and pressed around [Jesus]. And a woman was there who had been subject to bleeding for twelve years. She had suffered a great deal under the care of many doctors and had spent all she had, yet instead of getting better she grew worse. When she heard about Jesus, she came up behind him in the crowd and touched his cloak, because she thought, "If I just touch his clothes, I will be healed." Immediately her bleeding stopped and she felt in her body that she was freed from her suffering.*
>
> *At once Jesus realized that power had gone out from him.*[8]

One touch.

Twelve years of suffering submitted to one touch.

Research has shown that touch has the power to fight viruses, relieve stress, improve sleep, and help us recover more quickly from injury. One study done by a group of Utah researchers has found that a thirty-minute massage three times a week lowers levels of the stress-related enzyme alpha-amylase by 34 percent.[9] If you are married and your spouse hasn't read this book yet, you might want to underline that sentence and put it on his or her nightstand.

The power of touch, even on a human plane, is an amazing thing. But when you add the power of God to the equation, it sets the stage for something supernatural. The biblical practice of the laying on of hands is an endangered practice in too many church circles. We don't do it for a wide range of reasons. The church we grew up in didn't do it. It's a little too close for comfort. We don't realize that we're conduits of God's power. Or we simply don't believe in God's healing power. The result? Our lack of practice feeds our lack of faith.

Who knows how many miraculous moments we've forfeited because we've failed to act in a bold biblical fashion by praying for someone who is sick, commissioning someone who is called, or encouraging someone who just needs a hand on her shoulder?

The other night I felt impressed to pray for my younger son, Josiah. Our family gathered around him, laid hands on him, and prayed for him. I put my hand on his chest and prayed that Josiah would grow into the destiny of his name. He is named after the ancient Jewish king Josiah, who did what was right in the eyes of the Lord.[10] Later that night, after brushing his teeth and putting on his pajamas, Josiah innocently said, "Dad, I can't wait to grow up to be a king." Slight misinterpretation of my prayer! Lora asked me if I corrected him. Nope. Didn't have the heart.

Then my seven-year-old son said something that helped me appreciate an ancient biblical ritual in a way that no theologian could teach. He said, "Dad, have you done that hands thing with Parker and Summer?" Josiah was genuinely impacted by the simple fact that we had laid hands on him. He didn't get the terminology quite right or fully understand the biblical precedent, but he thought the laying on of hands was the coolest thing in the world. And it is. But it's more than cool.

We totally underestimate the power available to us as conduits of Christ, but every once in a while God gives us a glimpse. Almost like the golfer whose one good chip shot keeps his love for the game alive, there are those rare moments when we experience God's supernatural power and it keeps us believing for miracles! I had one of those moments a few years ago. But let me let the other person involved share the story from his perspective first.

For the first time in my life, I have recently started to experience the physical consequences of stress. I started a company with a friend of mine last year, and things are going well except that our former boss is suing us. I've never been sued by anyone, and we could be put out of business if we lose. Our arbitration proceeding began two weeks ago on a Monday. For the week prior to the arbitration, I was so stressed that my back cramped up on one side and became a source of constant pain. As the arbitration date drew closer, the pain got worse, but I assumed it would go away after the arbitration. The night before the arbitration there was a special service at NCC. And because of me, my wife and I were late. I drove as fast as I could and ended up getting a $150 speeding ticket on the way to church, making us more late! Toward the end of the service, you walked around to pray for people and you came to me first. And after you put your *hands on my head, and prayed for the Holy Spirit to fill me from head to toe, the pain in my back was gone. And it hasn't come back since. It's still mysterious to me, but all I know is what I experienced.*

Listen, my batting average when it comes to prayer is no better than anyone else's. And while I believe in divine healing, I don't consider it to be one of my spiritual gifts. But on the day of that healing miracle, I had been reading Luke 5:17:

And the power of the Lord was present for him to heal the sick.

As I spoke that night, the Holy Spirit surfaced that verse, and I sensed in my spirit that the power of the Lord was present to heal. So I followed the biblical prescription that hasn't changed in two thousand years: the laying on of hands.[11] And while this may not rank as the greatest miracle since Jesus stopped the issue of blood, I experienced a power surge just like Jesus. And that shouldn't surprise us, should it?

Anyone who has faith in me will do what I have been doing. He will do even greater things than these.[12]

SCIENCE FICTION

During a recent trip to Seattle, I spent an afternoon at the Science Fiction Museum. (After a pilgrimage to the original Starbucks at Pike Place Market, of course.) The museum was filled with lots of cool artifacts, but chief among them was Captain Kirk's chair from the starship *Enterprise*. I wouldn't call myself a Trekkie, but I loved the commission to "boldly go where no man has gone before." I actually had a toy phaser as a kid. And I've always loved those immortal words "Beam me up, Scotty."

As I toured the Science Fiction Museum, I couldn't help but notice that the things that capture our imagination are the things that are impossible but we wish they weren't. Dematerializing and rematerializing, for example. Fiction appeals to our highest hopes and deepest desires by depicting what we wish were true. That's why we love fiction.

So here's the good news: truth is stranger than fiction.

Jesus dematerialized and rematerialized. He stopped a tropical storm in its tracks. And He changed the molecular structure of water and turned it into wine. Jesus hard-wired a blind man's brain by installing synapses between the optic nerve and visual cortex. He defied the law of gravity. And He walked on water. Jesus walked through walls. He read minds. And He turned energy into matter by feeding five thousand with five loaves and two fish. Jesus made the blind see, the deaf hear, the mute talk, and the lame walk. And He didn't just raise people from the dead, He conquered death itself via His own resurrection.[13]

Now, here is the amazing thing: the same Spirit that raised Him from the dead is at work within us. The Holy Spirit is our sixth sense. He is also the fifth force.[14] He is the one who gives us extrasensory perception and supernatural power. Without Him, we can do nothing. With Him, all things are possible.[15]

Every once in a while, as I am speaking to our congregation or a group of leaders at a conference, I have a moment when I am absolutely overwhelmed by the cumulative potential of the people I'm speaking to. My mission in life, as a writer and pastor and parent, is to help people maximize their God-given potential. And that focus might fuel the feeling. But I often see things in people that they cannot see in themselves. I see churches in would-be church planters. I see books in would-be authors. I see CDs in would-be musicians. Of course, I'm guilty of seeing the worst in people too. But what would happen if we saw people through the eyes of God? I don't think we'd see their sin, because that is forgiven and forgotten. I think we'd see who they would, could, and should become in Christ. That is certainly the way God sees us.

GOD IS GOD

I have a prayer mantra. It's usually during a moment of weakness or a season of confusion that I utter this simple plea for help: "Lord, I can't do this in my own strength or wisdom." Have you ever been there? A pink slip or divorce filing or negative prognosis knocks the wind out of you. And you have no idea how you're going to make it through what you're going through. It's in those moments that I fall back on this primal truth: "Jesus loves me, this I know, for the Bible tells me so." Sometimes I'll even sing it.

There are enough failures dotting the landscape of my past to remind me of what I'm capable of. Or, I should say, incapable of. Most of what God accomplishes through our lives isn't *because* of us. It's *in spite* of us. I can't do what God has called me to do. Not in my own strength. But God never calls us to do something we're capable of. God calls us to do things that are beyond our ability so He gets all the credit. That's how we learn to rely on Him. And that's how we learn to love Him.

All of us love miracles. We just don't like being in situations where we need one. But that is a prerequisite. You will never experience the power of God until you put yourself into a situation that necessitates it. If you want to be filled with His Spirit, you don't have to walk a church aisle. Just walk into a situation that requires His power. Go after a God-ordained dream that cannot be accomplished in your own strength and wisdom.

I wonder how much of our spiritual activity boils down to managing God instead of seeking Him. Part of us wants a God that we can control. But there are moments in life—the loss of a loved one, a bad decision that comes back to haunt us, or a profound disappointment—that we cannot control. We lose control. But it's those moments that reveal an invaluable lesson. It ought to be the first thing we learn, but it's often the last thing we come to terms with: God is God. And by default, we're not.

I recently met Phil Vischer, the creator of VeggieTales. It was sort of surreal hearing the voice of Bob the Tomato in nonanimated form. But Phil is as likable as the characters he created.

Phil started out with loose change and grew Big Idea Inc. into a multimillion-dollar company that has sold more than fifty million videos. Over a three-year span during its heyday, revenues grew from $1.3 million to $44 million—that's an increase of 3,300 percent. But that all came to an end with one lawsuit. As Phil himself said, "Fourteen years' worth of work flashed before my eyes—the characters, the songs, the impact, the letters from kids all over the world. It all flashed before my eyes, then it all vanished."[16]

Big Idea declared bankruptcy. The dream died. And Phil was left to do some serious soul-searching. That's when Phil heard a sermon that saved his soul and changed his life. "If God gives you a dream, and the dream comes to life and God shows up in it, and then the dream dies, it may be that God wants to see what is more important to you—the dream or him."[17]

Let me ask you a question. It might be *the* question. Which do you love more: your dream or God? Do you love God for what He can do for you? Or do you love Him for who He is? In its purest, most primal form, loving God with all your heart, soul, mind, and strength is loving God for God. Nothing more. Nothing less. Nothing else.

In Phil's words, "The impact God has planned for us doesn't occur when we're pursuing impact. It occurs when we're pursuing God. At long last, after a lifetime of striving, God was enough. Not God and impact or God and ministry. Just God."[18]

Everything minus God equals nothing. God plus nothing equals everything. At the end of the day, all that matters is God. God is God. And the quest for our lost soul often begins when we get to the end of ourselves. But that is when life really begins.

We all want our lives to be about something bigger than us, more important than us, longer lasting than us. And that is exactly what God wants for you. But that isn't the ultimate goal. Loving God is. And if you learn to love God with all your heart, soul, mind, and strength, then your life will exceed your wildest expectations. Why? Because His love will be reflected in your life.

Isn't it time to stop serving your purposes and start serving His? Isn't it time to stop striving in your own strength and start flowing in His? Isn't it time to stop building your own kingdom and start advancing His?

You can put yourself on the throne of your life. You can try to get everyone to bow down and worship you. But you will run out of stuff to worship real quick and your universe will become smaller and smaller until the only thing that fits inside your tiny universe is you. But if you put God on the throne, your universe will get larger and larger. It will expand chronologically into eternity. It will expand experientially into heaven.

In the words of G. K. Chesterton, "How much happier you would be, how much more of you there would be, if the hammer of a higher God could smash your small cosmos."[19]

10

The Next Reformation

When God wants to initiate a new movement in history,
God does not intervene directly, but sends us dreams and
visions that can, if attended to, initiate the process.

—WALTER WINK

I was recently part of an international gathering of Christian leaders and
thinkers who met in Wittenberg, Germany, to discuss the state of
Christianity. The setting could not have been more apropos. It was there
that Martin Luther sparked the Protestant Reformation by nailing his
ninety-five theses to the doors of the Castle Church.

Our three-day conversation, which culminated on Reformation Day,
revolved around this question: do we need another reformation? The short
answer is yes. Every generation does. Every generation needs its Martin
Luthers, its Wittenbergs, and its ninety-five theses. But I don't think the
next reformation will look anything like the last reformation. A single
person won't lead it. A single event won't define it.

The last reformation was a reformation of creeds. The next reformation will be a reformation of deeds.[1] The last reformation was symbolized
by one central figure. The next reformation will be led by millions of
reformers living compassionately, creatively, and courageously for the
cause of Christ. It will be marked by broken hearts and sanctified imaginations. And the driving force will be the love of God. A love that is full
of compassion, wonder, curiosity, and energy.

HOLY RELICS

The last reformation dates back to the early sixteenth century. Pope Leo X was raising funds to build St. Peter's Basilica in Rome, and the primary means of fund-raising was indulgences. One of those fund-raisers, an itinerant preacher named Johann Tetzel, coined this catchy jingle: "As soon as the coin in the coffer rings, a soul from purgatory springs." In essence, salvation was for sale. And people were led to believe that each coin put into the coffer paid down time spent in purgatory.

By the year 1509, a depository of more than five thousand holy relics had been accumulated by Frederick the Wise, who wanted to make Wittenberg the Rome of Germany. The purported relics included a thorn from the crown of Christ, a twig from the burning bush, a piece of gold from the gift of the wise men, and a piece of bread from the Last Supper. The collection also included thousands of holy bones from dead saints. Each relic was given a chronological value. Viewing the bone of a dead saint, for example, was worth a reduction of four thousand years spent in purgatory. One of the silver coins paid to Judas? Fourteen hundred years. Add it all up, and the total value of the collection of holy relics was 1,902,202 years and 270 days.[2] Once a year, on All Saints' Day, all of those relics were put on display in Wittenberg, Germany. And it was the day before All Saints' Day, October 31, 1517, when one man challenged the status quo and changed the course of history.

No one knows where a reformation will begin or who will lead it. It often happens in unlikely places and is led by unlikely people. And a monk named Martin Luther was as unlikely a candidate as anybody.

Luther was a devout monk. Like the other monks in his order, he was awakened by the cloister bell at two o'clock in the morning and began the first of seven prayer cycles. His confessions lasted up to six hours. And he would often fast for three days on end without so much as a crumb of bread. Luther said of himself, "I was a good monk, and I kept the rule of my order so strictly that I may say that if ever a monk got to heaven by his monkery it was I."[3]

Then, in the fall of 1516, Martin Luther was teaching through the book of Romans at the University of Wittenberg when he came to this scripture: "The just shall live by faith." Luther experienced a theological tipping point. He said, "This passage of Paul became to me the gate of heaven."[4] And the rediscovery of a simple truth—*sola fide,* by faith alone—became the rallying cry of the Protestant Reformation.

Now let me make an all-important observation. If you miss this, you miss the soul of this book. Reformations are *not* born out of new discoveries. Those are often called cults. Reformations are born out of rediscovering something ancient, something primal. They are born out of primal truths rediscovered, reimagined, and radically reapplied to our lives.

So what does our generation need to rediscover? What primal truth needs to be reimagined? What is our reformation?

Simply put, we've got to be great at the Great Commandment. Anything less isn't good enough. Or, I should say, great enough. We must not succeed at the wrong thing. We must not invest our earthly lives in things that have no heavenly value. We must not be great at things that do not matter. We have to be great at what matters most. And what matters most is loving God with all our heart, soul, mind, and strength.

When you descend the flight of stairs into the soul of Christianity and everything is stripped away but its primal essence, what you're left with is the Great Commandment. Just as the medieval church rediscovered justification by faith, so our generation must rediscover the Great Commandment. The rallying cry of the last reformation was *"Sola fide."* The rallying cry of the next reformation is *"Amo Dei."*

Translation: "Love God."

SPIRITUAL LOVE LANGUAGE

Now let me make one final revelation: most of us have a natural bent toward one of the four dimensions of love. Think of it as your spiritual love language.[5] Maybe compassion comes easily because of the pain you've experienced in your own life. Or maybe your love language is wonder. You feel closer to God in the middle of creation than the middle of a church service. For some it's curiosity. Your spirit soars when your mind is stretched by a God idea. And for others, it's energy. You feel most fulfilled when you break a sweat for a kingdom cause.

I hope the idea of loving God in four ways isn't overwhelming. I hope it's exciting. I'm so grateful that God is big enough to be loved in so many different ways. Every relationship with God begins in the same way: at the foot of the cross. But then our lives become unique expressions of compassion, wonder, curiosity, and energy. And no one else can take your place. Oswald Chambers said, "Let God be as original with other people as He is with you."[6] I try to live by that premise. The way we love God will look very different based on our spiritual love language.

My primary spiritual love language is curiosity. I love learning new things. That's how I come alive. That's when I feel like I'm growing spiritually. Wonder is a close second. It's hard for me *not* to worship the Creator when I'm surrounded by His creation. That's the way I'm wired. And there is nothing wrong with playing to our strengths. So go ahead and love God in the way that comes most naturally to you. But you also need to cultivate the other love languages. Why? Because loving God in one way isn't enough. We're commanded to love Him with all our heart, soul, mind, and strength. And when we do, it's love to the fourth power.

Sometimes the greatest act of love isn't the one that comes most easily. It's the one that is most difficult or requires the greatest sacrifice. Maybe compassion or curiosity doesn't come as easily for you. If you learn to discipline yourself by practicing them, you'll find tremendous fulfillment in them. And God will be glorified.

Compassion, wonder, curiosity, and *energy* are nouns. It's our job to turn them into verbs. It's our highest calling and greatest privilege.

AMO DEI

The quest for the lost soul of Christianity in these pages is about to end, but I hope it's just begun in your life.

I hope this book has taken you back to some of the sympathy breakthroughs that have broken your heart and the epiphanies that have shaped your soul. I hope it's unleashed a holy curiosity to know God more. I hope it's renewed your resolve to devote your energies to kingdom causes. I hope this book has taken you down that flight of stairs, all the way back to the primal place where loving God with all your heart, soul, mind, and strength is all that matters.

I hope this book has been a torch. Now it's time for you to carry the torch. We've gone underground. Now it's time to go aboveground. We've descended the flight of stairs. Now it's time to ascend.

This book is an invitation to be part of something that is bigger than you, more important than you, and longer lasting than you. It's an invitation to be part of the next reformation. It's an invitation to be part of a primal movement that traces its origins all the way back to ancient catacombs where our spiritual ancestors were martyred because they loved God more than they loved life.

Amo Dei.

Notes

Chapter 1

1. Mark 12:30.

2. Since the time of Maimonides, a Spanish-born Jewish philosopher, the traditional number of Old Testament laws has been 613, comprising 248 positive commands and 365 negative commands.

3. Barna Group, "Most Twentysomethings Put Christianity on the Shelf Following Spiritually Active Teen Years," September 11, 2006, www .barna.org/barna-update/article/16-teensnext-gen/147-most-twenty somethings-put-christianity-on-the-shelf-following-spiritually-active-teen-years.

Chapter 2

1. Ezekiel 36:26.

2. For more information, check out www.thepeaceplan.com/.

3. Roger Thurow and Scott Kilman, *Enough: Why the World's Poorest Starve in an Age of Plenty* (New York: PublicAffairs, 2009), xiv; "Trends in Foster Care and Adoption—FY 2002–FY 2007," U.S. Department of Health and Human Services, Administration for Children and Families, www.acf.hhs.gov/programs/cb/stats_research/afcars/trends.htm; WikiAnswers.com, "How often do children die from drinking contaminated drinking water?" wiki.answers.com/Q/How_often_do _children_die_from_drinking_contaminated_drinking_water.

4. Quoted in Dacher Keltner, *Born to Be Good: The Science of a Meaningful Life* (New York: Norton, 2009), 225.

5. Keltner, *Born to Be Good,* 52.

6. Daniel Goleman, *Emotional Intelligence* (New York: Bantam, 1995), 34.

7. Genesis 37:2, NLT.

8. See Genesis 37:3–4.

9. Genesis 40:5–7, NLT.

10. Bill Hybels shares his unique angle on this story in his brilliant book *Holy Discontent: Fueling the Fire That Ignites Personal Vision* (Grand Rapids, MI: Zondervan, 2007), 45–46.

11. Check out www.tomsshoes.com/.

Chapter 3

1. Chip Heath and Dan Heath, *Made to Stick* (New York: Random House, 2007), 166–167.

2. Matthew 6:21.

3. Check out www.junkycarclub.com/.

4. Acts 2:45.

5. Gary Thomas, "Wise Christians Clip Obituaries," *Christianity Today,* October 3, 1994, www.christianitytoday.com/ct/1994/october3/4tb 024.html?start=1.

6. Jesus fed five thousand-plus people with five loaves of bread and two fish. And there were twelve baskets of leftovers. (See Luke 9:10–17.)

7. I have a timeworn, musty-smelling copy of J. C. Penney's autobiography, *Fifty Years with the Golden Rule,* on my shelf. It's worth the read.

8. See Mark 8:36.

9. To read more about the LA Dream Center, check out Matthew Barnett's book *The Church That Never Sleeps.*

10. I do believe this concept is in the Bible in the form of the thirty-, sixty-, and hundredfold blessing (see Matthew 13:23). God wants to multiply His blessings in our lives. There are certainly conditions, and the goal isn't personal prosperity. But if you genuinely give for the right reasons, God will bless it.

11. Check out www.compassion.com/.

12. Sanhedrin 37a.

Chapter 4

1. Genesis 1:31.
2. See Ephesians 3:20.
3. See Revelation 8:1.
4. Psalm 40:5, MSG.
5. Scott E. Hoezee, *Proclaim the Wonder: Engaging Science on Sunday* (Grand Rapids, MI: Baker, 2003), 222.
6. Psalm 29:1–2, 4–5, 7–9, MSG.
7. Oliver Sacks, *The Island of the Colorblind* (New York: Vintage Books, 1998), 36.
8. Sacks, *Island of the Colorblind,* 37–38.
9. Sacks, *Island of the Colorblind,* 208.
10. Elizabeth Barrett Browning, *Aurora Leigh,* bk. 7.
11. Proverbs 20:12.
12. John Stevens, quoted in David N. Menton, "The Eye," 1991, http://emporium.turnpike.net/C/cs/eye.htm.
13. 1 Corinthians 2:9–10.
14. Greg Stielstra, *PyroMarketing: The Four-Step Strategy to Ignite Customer Evangelists and Keep Them for Life* (New York: HarperBusiness, 2005), 92.
15. Matthew 6:22–23, MSG.
16. Genesis 28:12, 16–17.
17. 1 Peter 1:18, MSG.

Chapter 5

1. Lawrence Kushner, *Eyes Remade for Wonder* (Woodstock, VT: Jewish Lights, 1998), 50.
2. See Job 33:14.
3. Jesus used variations of this phrase repeatedly. (See Matthew 11:15; 13:9, 43; Mark 4:9, 23; Luke 8:8; 14:35; Revelation 2:7, 11, 17, 29; 3:6, 13, 22; 13:9.)

4. Thanks to Andy Stanley for this thought. I'm paraphrasing something I heard him say. By the way, he's one of my favorite pastors and preachers. You ought to check out his podcasts at www.northpoint.org/podcasts.

5. Dorothy L. Sayers, *Creed or Chaos?* (Manchester, NH: Sophia Institute Press, 1995), 5.

6. Psalm 119:99.

7. *The Autobiography of Nathaniel Southgate Shaler, with a Supplementary Memoir by His Wife* (Boston: Houghton Mifflin, 1909), 98–100.

8. Bodil Jönsson, *Unwinding the Clock: Ten Thoughts on Our Relationship to Time,* trans. Tina Nunnally (New York: Harcourt, 2001), 16.

9. AOL CityGuide, 2008.

10. James 1:22–25.

11. A18 is a shortened reference to this verse, Acts 1:8.

Chapter 6

1. "Taxi Drivers' Brains 'Grow' on the Job," BBC News, March 14, 2000, http://news.bbc.co.uk/1/hi/sci/tech/677048.stm.

2. For additional research on plasticity, check out Peter R. Huttenlocher, *Neural Plasticity: The Effects of Environment on the Development of the Cerebral Cortex* (Cambridge: Harvard University Press, 2002).

3. 1 Corinthians 8:2.

4. Neuropsychologists Vinod Goel and Raymond Dolan define humor as "a cognitive juxtaposition of mental sets." See www.pubmedcentral.nih.gov/articlerender.fcgi?artid=2631939.

5. I've heard estimates that are lower than this, but two seems to be the consensus. For what it's worth, I just listened to a *Success Magazine* CD that cites a study about CEOs. The average CEO reads four or five books per month. And for the record, they earn 536 times as much income as the average person.

6. Ronald W. Clark, *Einstein: The Life and Times* (New York: Avon, 1984), 755.

7. Quoted in Scott Thorpe, *How to Think like Einstein: Simple Ways to Break the Rules and Discover Your Hidden Genius* (Naperville, IL: Sourcebooks, 2000), 115.

8. Michael J. Gelb, *How to Think like Leonardo da Vinci: Seven Steps to Genius Every Day* (New York: Delacorte, 1998), 65.

9. Genesis 1:28.

10. Pneumatology is theology of the Holy Spirit. Soteriology is theology of salvation. Eschatology is theology of the end times.

11. 1 Kings 4:29, 32–34.

12. Proverbs 25:2.

13. *The Works of Francis Bacon,* ed. Basil Montagu, 3 vols. (Philadelphia: Carey and Hart, 1844), 1:176.

14. Thanks to A. W. Tozer for this thought.

15. See http://imagine.gsfc.nasa.gov/docs/ask_astro/answers/0211 27a.html.

16. The TED conference is a gathering of innovative leaders from a variety of disciplines, such as business, science, entertainment, and the nonprofit sector (www.TED.com).

17. Richard Restak, *Mozart's Brain and the Fighter Pilot: Unleashing Your Brain's Potential* (New York: Harmony, 2001), 92.

18. John 4:22, NLT and NIV.

19. John 4:24.

20. Russell Stannard, *The God Experiment: Can Science Prove the Existence of God?* (Mahwah, NJ: HiddenSpring, 2000), 77.

21. I'm aware that we disagree on what those nonnegotiables are. And it's hard to know where to draw that line. If you'd like to examine NCC's core belief statement, visit www.theaterchurch .com.

22. Gelb, *How to Think like Leonardo da Vinci,* 50.

23. See Matthew 7:7–8.

24. Gelb, *How to Think like Leonardo da Vinci,* 38.

Chapter 7

1. Either the mind of God or the mind of man.
2. See Psalm 33:3; 96:1; 98:1; 144:9; 149:1.
3. See Ephesians 3:20.
4. Ian C. Bradley, *The Celtic Way* (London: Darton, Longman, and Todd, 2003), 98.
5. Check out http://rethinkmonthly.com/2009/06/mark-batterson-what -are-you-rethinking/.
6. See the cameo at www.thepotteries.org/did_you/005.htm.
7. See http://wedgwoodcircle.com/why_wedgwood/ and Philippians 4:8.
8. 2 Corinthians 10:5.
9. See 1 Kings 5–6.
10. 1 Chronicles 28:11–12.
11. Colossians 4:2.
12. Warren G. Bennis and Robert J. Thomas, *Geeks and Geezers: How Era, Values, and Defining Moments Shape Leaders* (Boston: Harvard Business School Press, 2002), 19.
13. The Aramaic word is *slotha*.
14. See Habakkuk 2:2.
15. Check out www.markbatterson.com.
16. Arthur McKinsey, quoted in M. Mitchell Waldrop, *Complexity: The Emerging Science at the Edge of Order and Chaos* (New York: Simon and Schuster, 1992), 29.
17. Habakkuk 2:1, NLT.
18. Quoted at www.heroesofhistory.com/page11.html.
19. Quoted in Marion Owen, "For the Love of Peanuts," http://www .plantea.com/love-peanuts.htm.
20. See www.quotationspage.com/quote/8924.html.
21. Yann Martel, quoted in Kent D. Curry, "A Piece of the Pi," *Relevant,* May–June 2009, 87.

Chapter 8

1. Matthew 25:21, 23.
2. Malcolm Gladwell, *Outliers: The Story of Success* (New York: Little, Brown, 2008), 249.
3. Check out *Talent Is Overrated: What Really Separates World-Class Performers from Everybody Else,* by Geoff Colvin, in addition to *Outliers,* by Malcolm Gladwell.
4. Gladwell, *Outliers,* 41.
5. Matthew 28:19.
6. See James 2:14–26.
7. This concept (along with many others, I'm sure) was inspired by John Maxwell.
8. Matthew 25:26.
9. Dorothy Sayers, "The Greatest Drama Ever Staged," in *Letters to a Diminished Church* (Nashville: W Publishing Group, 2004).
10. John 2:17, NLT.
11. John 4:31–34.
12. Proverbs 29:18, KJV.
13. See Philippians 1:6.

Chapter 9

1. See Acts 1:8.
2. Isaiah 55:8–9 compares the difference between our thoughts and God's thoughts to the expanse of the universe.
3. 1 John 1:5.
4. Romans 12:1, MSG.
5. Genesis 1:3.
6. See Isaiah 55:11, KJV.
7. Psalm 33:6, 9.
8. Mark 5:24–30.
9. "Let Your Hands Do the Talking," *Men's Health,* April 2009.
10. See 2 Kings 22–23.

11. See Luke 4:40.

12. John 14:12.

13. For the miracles in the order I have listed them, see John 20:19; Mark 4:35–41; John 2:1–11; 9:6–11; Acts 1:9; Matthew 14:22–33; John 20:19, 26; Matthew 12:25; Luke 9:10–17; 7:22; and Matthew 28.

14. Some physicists postulate the existence of a fifth force in addition to the four forces of nature: gravity, electromagnetism, the strong nuclear force, and the weak nuclear force.

15. See Matthew 19:26.

16. Phil Vischer, *Me, Myself, and Bob: A True Story About God, Dreams, and Talking Vegetables* (Nashville: Nelson, 2006), 196.

17. Vischer, *Me, Myself, and Bob,* 234.

18. Vischer, *Me, Myself, and Bob,* 246.

19. G. K. Chesterton, *Orthodoxy* (Sioux Falls, SD: NuVision, 2007), 18.

Chapter 10

1. Thanks to Rick Warren for this thought and for modeling it with his life.

2. Roland H. Bainton, *Here I Stand: A Life of Martin Luther* (New York: Meridian, 1995), 53.

3. Bainton, *Here I Stand,* 34.

4. Bainton, *Here I Stand,* 50.

5. Thanks to Gary Chapman for this language. I'm applying his phrase, "love languages," to our relationship with God. If you haven't read *The Five Love Languages,* I highly recommend it.

6. Oswald Chambers, *My Utmost for His Highest* (New York: Dodd, Mead, 1935), June 13.